THE
AMERICAN
SHAKESPEARE
FESTIVAL

The Birth of a Theatre

by

JOHN HOUSEMAN AND JACK LANDAU

Simon and Schuster · *New York*

1959

CONTENTS

"Curtain going up!" — *August 1958*

The Vision

Dᴜʀɪɴɢ the weekend ending September 14, 1958, the American Shakespeare Festival Theatre gave the final performances of its fourth repertory season. This brought to twelve the number of Shakespeare's plays produced at Stratford, Connecticut, for audiences totaling over half a million people...

*"I pray you tarry. Pause a day or two
Before you hazard; for, in choosing wrong,
I lose your company . . ."*

Morris Carnovsky as Shylock

8

THE MERCHANT OF VENICE

KATHARINE
HEPBURN
as Portia

MEASURE FOR MEASURE

[*Opposite*]
Vienna — an apartment in the Duke's Palace

[*Above left*]
Kent Smith as Angelo and Nina Foch as Isabella

[*Above right*]
"*Sweet sister, let me live.*" — Donald Harron as Claudio

[*Right*]
Whitford Kane as Abhorson, Hiram Sherman as
Pompey

[*Below*]
"*O heavens! what stuff is here?*" Arnold Moss as
the Duke

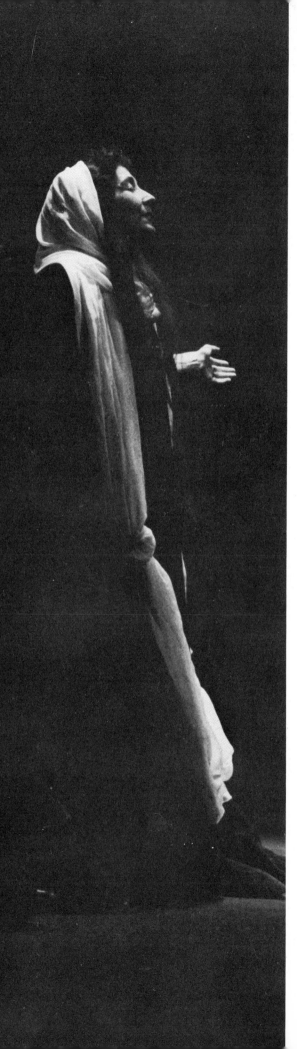

KING JOHN

[*Left*]
MILDRED DUNNOCK as Constance

[*Below*]
"And then all this thou seest is but a clod
And module of confounded royalty."

[*Opposite top*]
JOHN EMERY as King John, FRITZ WEAVER as Faulconbridge

[*Opposite bottom*]
PERNELL ROBERTS as Pembroke, EARLE HYMAN as Melun,
PATRICK HINES as Bigot, MORRIS CARNOVSKY as Salisbury

"... the isle is full of noises,
Sounds and sweet airs, that
give delight and hurt not."

RAYMOND MASSEY as Prospero

THE TEMPEST

14

OTHELLO

[Below]
ALFRED DRAKE as Iago, RICHARD EASTON
as Roderigo

[Right]
*"He takes her by the palm;
ay, well said, whisper."*

[Bottom]
*" . . . O my soul's joy!
If after every tempest come such calms,
May the winds blow till they have wakened
    death!"*

JACQUELINE BROOKES as Desdemona, EARLE
HYMAN as Othello, RICHARD WARING as Cassio

NINA FOCH as Katherina, MORRIS CARNOVSKY as Grumio and
PERNELL ROBERTS as Petruchio

THE TAMING OF THE SHREW

"What, will my daughter prove a good musician?"
PATRICK HINES as Baptista, PERNELL ROBERTS as Petruchio,
KENDALL CLARK as Hortensio, and FRITZ WEAVER as Gremio.
Above, MIKE KELLIN as Christopher Sly

RODDY McDOWALL
as
Octavius Caesar

LEORA DANA as Portia and RAYMOND MASSEY as Brutus

CHRISTOPHER PLUMMER
as
Marcus Antonius

JULIUS CAESAR

"Liberty! Freedom! Tyranny is dead!"
HURD HATFIELD as Julius Caesar

17

The Play-Scene: INGA SWENSON as Ophelia and FRITZ WEAVER as Hamlet

"O! Speak to me no more;
These words like daggers enter in mine ears.
No more,
Sweet Hamlet!"

18

HAMLET

Barbara Barrie as the Player Queen and Ellis Rabb as the Player King

Morris Carnovsky as Claudius, Geraldine Fitzgerald as Gertrude, Inga Swenson as Ophelia and Hiram Sherman as Polonius

19

[*Above*]
BENEDICK: "I pray you, what is he?"
BEATRICE: "Why, he is the Prince's jester, a very dull fool . . ."

[*Opposite top*]
The wedding: MORRIS CARNOVSKY as Antonio, KATHARINE HEPBURN as Beatrice, JOHN COLICOS as Leonato, LOIS NETTLETON as Hero, KENDALL CLARK as Friar Francis, RICHARD EASTON as Claudio, ALFRED DRAKE as Benedick and STANLEY BELL as Don Pedro

[*Opposite bottom*]
"Bring him away. O that I had been writ down an ass!"
> WILLIAM COTTRELL as Oatcake, MITCHELL AGRUSS as Conrade, JACK BITTNER as Borachio, DONALD HARRON as Verges, LARRY GATES as Dogberry

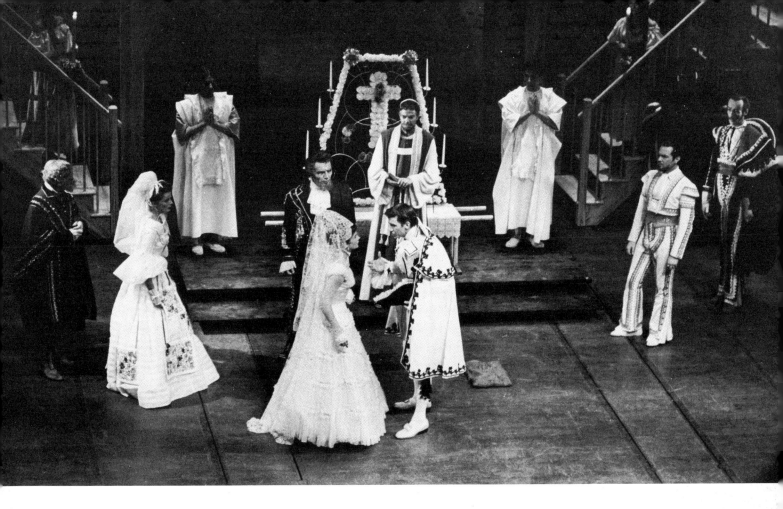

MUCH ADO ABOUT NOTHING

THE WINTER'S TALE

[*Left*]
"Get you hence for I must go."
BARBARA BARRIE as Dorcas, EARLE HYMAN as Autolycus and JUNE ERICSON as Mopsa. Behind them, WILL GEER as the Old Shepherd

[*Opposite*]
JAMES OLSON as Archidamus, RICHARD WARING as Polixenes and ELLIS RABB as Camillo "in Bohemia."

*". . . be stone no more; approach.
Strike all that look upon with marvel."*
RICHARD WARING as Polixenes, NANCY MARCHAND as Paulina, NANCY WICKWIRE as Hermione, JOHN COLICOS as Leontes, RICHARD EASTON as Florizel, INGA SWENSON as Perdita and MITCHELL AGRUSS as Angelo

" . . . *Reverend sirs,*
For you there's rosemary and rue; these keep
Seeming and savour all the winter long."

Act I, Theseus' Palace. NANCY WICKWIRE as Hippolyta, JOHN COLICOS as Lysander, JAMES OLSON as Demetrius, BARBARA BARRIE as Hermia, PATRICK HINES as Egeus and JACK BITTNER as Theseus. In the back, EARLE HYMAN as Philostrate; on the balcony, RUSSELL OBERLIN as the Master of the Revels

" . . . *Sing me now asleep;*
Then to your offices, and let me rest."
JUNE HAVOC as Titania with her elves

"*O when she's angry, she is keen and shrewd!*"
Demetrius, Hermia and Lysander

A MIDSUMMER NIGHT'S DREAM

"Thou wall, O wall, O sweet and lovely wall!"

WILLIAM HICKEY as Flute

"The Rude Mechanicals"

HIRAM SHERMAN as Bottom

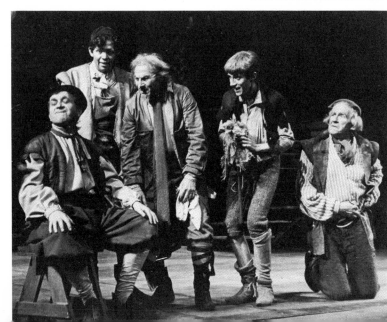

WILL GEER as Snout

6:30 P.M.

6:45 P.M.

A<small>T ITS</small> final matinee, with the clowns stretching their scenes and the audience in a sentimental mood, *A Midsummer Night's Dream* ran several minutes longer than usual, and it was after six o'clock when the last of the fairy train vanished into the stage floor. Almost before the theatre was empty, the stage-crew took over. By midnight, scenery, costumes and props for *Dream, Hamlet* and *The Winter's Tale* had been struck and stored. Another Festival season was over.

27

LAWRENCE LANGNER

Five years earlier, where the Festival Theatre now stands, there had been only waste lots running down to the Housatonic River. Five years before that the Festival itself was no more than a dream in Lawrence Langner's head.

This was his vision:

"The Theatre that will be built to house Shakespeare's plays will be patterned after the old Globe Theatre in London, and will have approximately 1,600 seats. It will, however, include every appropriate improvement that has been developed since, making it possible to adapt it to any kind of production—Elizabethan or modern.

"It is planned that the Festival shall begin in June and run, at first, for a period of ten weeks. Then during the winter the Acting Company will travel on an extended tour throughout the country. The fact that the plays will be played in the summer and under summer conditions will make it possible, once again, to produce Shakespeare's plays in the American theatre.

"The Academy, which will form an important part of the organization, will be located in the theatre building or buildings. Particular emphasis will be placed upon the training of actors in the style of acting best suited to performing the works of Shakespeare in the United States."

SINCE this statement was published by Lawrence Langner in 1950, the American Shakespeare Festival Theatre and Academy (ASFTA) has undergone many personal and material changes. Yet, for all the conflicts and compromises, the happy surprises and the hopes deferred, the original aims expressed by its founder almost a decade ago have not substantially altered. The Theatre, the Acting Company and the Academy— these are and always will be the three essential elements of the Festival's operation.

Of the three Stratfords, Connecticut's is the youngest— in function if not in conception. Warwickshire has had a Memorial Theatre since 1861; the Ontario Festival was founded in 1953. The opening of the Festival theatre at Stratford, Connecticut, in July 1955 was the consummation of the efforts of hundreds of workers over a period of more than four years.

It was in 1951 that Langner engaged Edwin L. Howard, Westport architect, to draw up the first of a series of theatre designs on which they were to work together for the next four years. Offices and a fund-raising staff were established in Westport and in the Theatre Guild in New York. Then, with the aid of Kenneth Bradley of Bridgeport, a bill was prepared and presented to the Connecticut State Legislature establishing the American Shakespeare Festival Theatre and Academy as a non-profit, educational corporation in that state. It was signed on June 9, 1951, by Governor John Lodge, himself a former actor.

With the granting of the charter and the reaction in the local and New York press, the work of organizing and financing the Festival began. Under the leadership of Helen Menken in New York and Marienne Chatin of Greenwich, Connecticut, working committees were formed locally and in places as far afield as Boston, Philadelphia, Wilmington, Baltimore and Washington. To stimulate interest in the new venture an entertainment was presented consisting of scenes from Shakespeare's plays, produced by Mary Hunter, staged by Margaret Webster, and performed by a company of well-known theatrical stars. "An Evening with Will Shakespeare" opened in Hartford and played a six-week tour of major Eastern cities. Meantime, Lawrence Langner had persuaded Lewis W. Douglas, former Ambassador to Great Britain, to become National Chairman of the organization. With his endorsement of the project, it was possible to secure the interest of the Rockefeller Foundation, which promised $300,000, provided an equal sum was raised from other sources.

During 1954 two new names were added to the Board of Trustees— Lincoln Kirstein, founder of the New York City Ballet, and Joseph Verner Reed, long a generous supporter of the performing arts. With their aid the project took on an accelerated motion; a visit to Paul Mellon in Washington resulted in the Old Dominion Foundation matching the Rockefeller grant. With these two massive contributions added to those received from other foundations, from some 3,000 members of the public and from ASFTA Trustees including Helen Menken, George N. Richard and Roger Stevens, the Festival dream seemed finally on its way to realization.

Fund raising, however, was not the only problem the founders had to face. For months, stretching into years, a search was under way for a suitable site on which to erect the theatre, its Academy and administrative buildings. A committee of Connecticut real-estate agents submitted over one hundred locations, of which more than fifty were visited by Lawrence Langner and, for

Miss Helen Menken and Lincoln Kirstein

Joseph Verner Reed

29

one reason or another, found unsatisfactory. When an excellent site was discovered in Westport and made available by the state of Connecticut at a reasonable price, local property owners circulated a petition against the erection of a theatre in their midst. Similar civic opposition was encountered in five other townships including, at first, Stratford, Connecticut, which the Trustees now favored as the site of the Festival.

Heartened by the support of the local press (notably Paul Deegan of the Stratford *News* and Ethel Beckwith of the Bridgeport *Herald*) the quest continued— until one spring day in 1954, when members of the Building Committee were invited to inspect a site on the banks of the Housatonic. The group, guided by Mrs. W. Forrest Davenport, owner of a contiguous property, enjoyed a picnic and admired the river view. The location was unanimously approved and a sum of $60,000 was donated by the directors of the Theatre Guild (Lawrence Langner, Theresa Helburn and Armina Marshall) for its acquisition. Two months later, after cautiously conducted negotiations, the Trustees proudly announced that they had obtained ownership of the four pieces of land on which the Festival Theatre and its Academy now stand.

On October 24, 1954, the ground-breaking took place in the presence of several hundred persons. As the press reported:

"With the setting sun as a spotlight, and the green, russet and gold foliage of autumn as a backdrop, Miss Katharine Cornell used a gilded shovel adorned with green ribbons to turn up a section of the soil on which the original founders of the town of Stratford disembarked from England in the year 1639."

30

April 1954:
Where the theatre now stands there were . . . waste lots along the Housatonic River

Edwin Howard, meantime, had drafted no less than five separate architectural designs for the building, making different versions to conform to the constantly shifting sites and changing notions of what the Festival theatre should be— including the trustees' final decision to make it "an all-year building which could also house ballet, symphony concerts and a wide variety of stage presentations." This and other developments had brought the estimated cost of the project from five to eight hundred thousand and then eventually to more than a million dollars.

That such a sum could be raised without federal, state or municipal help for a project that was still little more than a hope is a tribute to that haphazard but miraculous combination of personal initiative, private generosity and organized munificence which characterizes U. S. cultural life in our time. Three quarters of a million dollars were donated by foundations; private contributions totaled over half a million in amounts ranging from two dollars to the quarter of a million contributed by Joseph Verner Reed. Other gifts included shrubs, trees, electrical equipment, rent-free premises in New York, paintings, thirty thousand feet of Guiana teakwood from the Government of the French Republic and the proceeds from a diversity of theatrical benefits.

Early in 1955, the Festival began to take concrete shape with the erection of the theatre. Working closely with Edwin Howard, Alice Orme Smith, a well-known landscape artist, had planned the exact site of the building in relation to existing trees, grades and river front. On January 1, 1955, work began.

The first daily report to the builder, Walter Binger, from his superintendent, Theodore Dachenhausen, shows that on that

31

Maurice Evans, Stratford Councilman D. James Morey and Miss Katharine Cornell

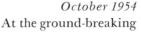

October 1954
At the ground-breaking

1951–1955: Architect Edwin Howard drafted five separate designs to conform to the shifting sights and changing notion of what the Festival Theatre should be.

day, in snowy, very cold weather, two bulldozers moved "into the lobby area," stripping and stacking topsoil that was frozen twelve inches deep. Four days later work was stopped, owing to the cold.

"February 3: Cold weather. Shovel bucket and blade of bulldozer damaged yesterday due to frozen ground. They repaired same today and will resume work on Monday."

The following week they were excavating the stage and "filling in old pond area with what was dug out of the hole." That day they poured the first concrete, even though, "due to wet weather and deep mud, trucks were constantly getting stuck."

"February 17: Half of lobby walls poured today and about one half of rear footing of stage area.

"February 18: Weather ideal for concrete work and will make the most of it.

"February 23: Rain.

"February 28: Poured the biggest part of the north foundation wall and the east footings of stage area.

"March 1: Rain. Erected steel reinforcing of west end.

"March 9: Poured the west wall of stage area today. Now installing forms for the orchestra section and starting a footing for east side of auditorium.

"March 11: We are all ready for steel which will come early Tuesday. Carpenters next.

"March 16: Set the lobby flat steel but forced away by rain.

"April 1: Carpenters have lobby beams almost in. They started on wood bearings in stage area. Plumbers on strike."

From the daily reports it appears that during April, as the theatre began to take shape, the superintendent began to lose his equanimity. His reports have a nervous tone which the Rooftree Raising on May 15 (attended by such notables as Walter Hampden, Ezio Pinza, Maurice Evans, Myrna Loy and Brian Aherne) failed to allay.

"All the small contracts must be let . . . Everyone is busy . . . The longer we wait, the worse it gets.

"Steel is so slow. Carpentry is definitely behind.

"Somehow someone has fouled up on the insulation. . . . Everyone knows that the heat loss is through the roof.

The Building Superintendent reports . . .

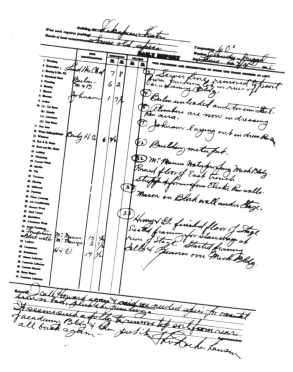

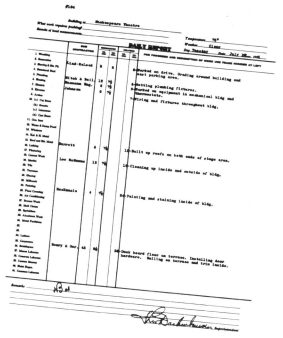

33

January 1955 . . .

"The time is getting shorter and shorter.

"We cannot wait on people who take three days to a week to make a decision . . . from now on, no more changes.

"So much left to do and no time left to do it.

"I fear for July 12."

If the building superintendent was worried about the opening of the Festival on July 12, he was not alone. The ASFTA Board of Trustees and more particularly the members of its

Executive Committee were worried too. With the planning, financing and erection of the theatre, they had achieved their first objective. The Festival had a home. To this extent the dream was realized, and the man who was its prime mover hailed the new structure as "a triumph of our national pride . . . one which will mean many things to many people. To some it will mean a place where they will go to refresh their minds and spirits, to drink deeply at the eternal fountain which is Shakespeare. To others it will mean the sheer magic of the theatre brought to them by great stars in great roles in great plays."

. . . July 1955

[*Left to right*]
WALTER BINGER (builder), ARMINA MARSHALL, LAWRENCE LANGNER, MRS. ROGER STEVENS, MAURICE EVANS, ROGER STEVENS, JEAN ROSENTHAL and EDWIN HOWARD (architect). After many meetings . . .

. . . the Rooftree Raising. "A triumph of our national pride — one that will mean many things to many people."

H ERE precisely lay the critical problem now facing the trustees of the American Shakespeare Festival. Still incredulous and breathless from the effort of their great material accomplishment— the first full-scale professional playhouse to be built in the United States in a quarter of a century— they now found themselves faced with the even harder task of hurriedly assembling actors to play in it and a public to patronize it. In less than three months they had to meet the many challenges inevitably facing the founders of an American classical repertory theatre— dangerous and complex problems of style and tradition, attitude and personnel. The story of how, three years later, these problems were still being met is told in two later sections of this book.

In March 1955, ASFTA announced its choice of plays— *Julius Caesar* and *The Tempest*— and the appointment of a director, Denis Carey of the Bristol (England) Old Vic. In the weeks that followed, designers were named, stars and a company signed and announced. Rehearsals were conducted, first in New York and then in Stratford's Cupheag Social Club over the Lovell Hardware Store. The stage itself was made available to the company for a total of thirty-four hours, which included two dress rehearsals, punctuated by riveting and similar interruptions.

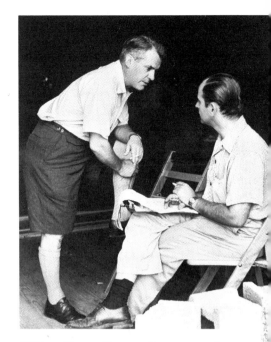

1955: — DENIS CAREY, director, and PETER ZEISLER, stage manager

The U. S. correspondent of the London *Daily Telegraph and Morning Post* reported:

"Stratford, Connecticut, July 8: There are less than 120 hours to go and the building is still under construction. When I visited the theatre today, a small army of about a hundred carpenters, electricians, masons, and plumbers were laboring with a zeal that was not only gratifying to its organizers but which, no doubt, would have pleased Shakespeare himself. Many of them were stripped to the waist."

On July 12— the day *Julius Caesar* was to open— as cast, director and crew were bracing themselves for the ordeal of inaugurating the American Shakespeare Festival before a distinguished but skeptical first-night audience, the superintendent reported the following building trades still at work on the structure: carpentry, painting, cement work, roofing and sheet metal, electric, heating, plumbing and excavation! Nevertheless, the opening performance of *Julius Caesar* did take place as scheduled, accompanied by speeches and congratulatory telegrams from Dwight D. Eisenhower and Winston Churchill, who hailed this newest Stratford Festival as "completing the three sides of the Triangle."

37

July 12, 1955 — OPENING NIGHT

On hand for the event, besides numerous well-known theatrical figures, was a capacity audience that included (above, left to right) the Mayor of Stratford-upon-Avon, in his traditional black robes and chain of office, Sir Roger Makins, British Ambassador to the U.S., Governor Ribicoff of Connecticut and U.S. Senator Prescott Bush, who posed with Lawrence Langner in front of the "Chesterfield" portrait of Shakespeare by Gerard von Soest. Sharing a box with Episcopal Bishop Grey of Connecticut was a correspondent of the Soviet news service, Tass (opposite, top right), whose presence, first banned and then, at the last moment, authorized by the U.S. Department of State, made him suddenly the most newsworthy item of the evening.   39

Julius Caesar was followed on August 1 by *The Tempest* and, a month later, by a student production of *Much Ado about Nothing*. But work on the theatre did not cease with the opening of the plays; it continued, on a diminishing scale, until September 16, two weeks after the close of the season. On that date, the superintendent reported, "Contract completed."

THERE it stands, blending gradually into the New England countryside, the stagehouse rising tall and clear above the surrounding fields, the old clapboard houses and the brand-new aircraft plants across the Housatonic River. Of the original Globe Theatre conception, little is left beyond the theatre's octagonal form and its decorative use of natural wood. Terraces have been added, also lawns, shrubs and trees; on its western face a huge painted sundial has been affixed— the only sundial in the world to mark Eastern Daylight Saving Time. With the years, certain native characteristics of the building have become apparent. With its high, delicate lantern and its long gray surfaces, the Festival theatre has more in common with the local meetinghouses and tobacco barns than with the heavy timber of the Elizabethan builders. "It's a bastard!" is one colleague's comment cheerfully quoted by its architect, Edwin Howard. A leading New York drama critic has described it as "the most beautiful, comfortable playhouse I have ever been in— the perfect theatre!"

Functionally, inside and out, the Stratford playhouse has proved itself well suited to the conditions of Festival theatre-

40

going and flexible enough to satisfy all the material and aesthetic demands that have been made on it. In its combination of modernity and tradition it fittingly represents the spirit of the organization whose concrete symbol it is.

The American Shakespeare Festival Theatre and Academy was conceived, built and manned in pursuit of a vision that has come closer to realization, in a shorter time, than its founders ever dared to hope. In the four years of its existence it has won a large measure of critical and popular acceptance. Annual attendance has risen from an estimated sixty-five thousand in 1955 to over one hundred and fifty thousand in the summer of 1958. It is on such steadily growing support that the ASFTA governing board bases its faith in a future that promises far more than the efficient operation of a summer festival or the maintenance of a repository for respected educational exhibits:

"We are well aware that in attempting to create this kind of theatre, at this particular time, we have assumed an unusual responsibility and must meet a special challenge. We believe that a Classical Repertory Company performing successfully for more than four months of the year, within 90 minutes of Broadway and with the whole nation as its ultimate audience, is supplying a pressing cultural need and fulfilling an essential function in contemporary American life."

41

1951 — "A decidedly Tudor feeling . . ."
project by EDWIN HOWARD

1955 — Julius Caesar, Act I, Scene 1
Designed by HORACE ARMISTEAD

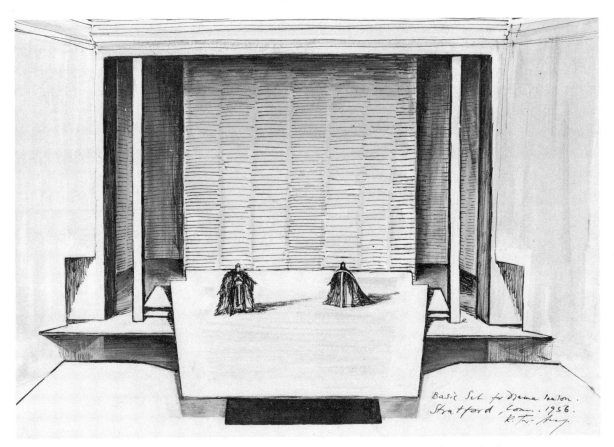

1956 — The Festival Stage
Designed by ROUBEN TER-ARUTUNIAN

· II ·

Stage and Style

1955-1958

Vᴉꜱɪᴛᴏʀꜱ to the American Shakespeare Festival are usually struck by three things: first, the obvious attractions of its natural location— the lawns, the river view, the picnic tables under the trees; second, the spacious and handsome theatre—its wood-lined auditorium and the three paneled lobbies whose walls are covered with the paintings and engravings of what is becoming one of the country's finest classical-theatre collections; third and last, the stage— the heart of the Festival— which has grown, with the years, into an instrument of great originality and resource. 43

1955: THE FIRST STAGE

OF THE Festival stage, in its original form, the architect has written:

"A copy of Shakespeare's Globe never was planned, but our first sketches had a decidedly Tudor feeling which was integral to the problem of including an Elizabethan type of stage. After many conferences with various experts in the theatrical field, it was decided to design the building so that plays could be presented in a variety of ways— either with a fixed Elizabethan set or with sets on wagons for quick repertory use, or with sets hung above the stage in the modern manner. The stagehouse took form with a high central portion for the big sets and lower side spaces for the wagons. The forestage was designed so that it could extend the entire width of the auditorium (92 ft.) or could be cut down to the size of the proscenium opening (45 ft.). It can extend out into the audience or be removed to allow for a large orchestra pit for musical productions. To assist in an unbroken continuity between audience and actors, there are side galleries outside the proscenium. If the forestage is not used, the picture-frame proscenium can be installed to separate the auditorium from the stage."

This design was consistent with the trustees' desire for a stage that would adjust to almost any style or mode of Shakespearean production and which, in between Festival seasons, would be capable of accommodating opera, ballet and symphony orchestras, contemporary drama as well as musical comedy. And this was the huge, carefully planned and elaborately equipped stage plant which confronted Denis Carey, the director, Horace Armistead, the scenic artist, Robert Fletcher, the costume designer, and Jean Rosenthal, the lighting and production expert, as they envisaged their first Festival season. Designs and schemes, sketches and hanging plots, building and painting, rehearsals and fittings— all these preparations, of necessity, took place in New York, 65 miles from the scaffolded building at Stratford, of which nothing was known beyond its physical dimensions: nothing of its virtues or perils, nothing of its aural or visual dynamics, nothing of its effect on the actors who would be working in it or of their relation to the spectators before whom they would have to play.

Arriving in Stratford before the building was completed, with a company champing to be let loose on the vast acreage of stage that had been promised, Carey and his colleagues found, in addition to the elegant teak-finished auditorium: *(a)* a proscenium opening that seemed even larger than it was; *(b)* a "wooden O" with excellent acoustics; *(c)* a stagehouse of magnificent proportions but with a still unresolved relation between stage and audience; *(d)* a vast forestage with connected sidestages, above which rose two tiers of Elizabethan galleries, providing opportunity for lateral action on many levels.

The organic use of this new theatre presented serious problems to its first occupants. All the more since there was so little time to investigate and adjust the thorny problems of production to the magnificent resources implicit in the design. The result was uneven but illuminating.

According to Lincoln Kirstein:

"From the beginning of the Connecticut venture, the underlying philosophy was a devotion to the intention of the author. What Shakespeare intended in *Julius Caesar* was a vision of Rome in crisis;

Julius Caesar, Act III, Scene 1

45

for him the past was simultaneous; it was an immediate rather than an archaeological past. When Shakespeare thought of a Senator, of honest Brutus and lean and hungry Cassius, did he have togas in mind? It is unlikely. Then what *did* he see in his mind's eye as the clothing and building of republican Rome? What were his sources? For history, we know that he had North's translation of Plutarch. For architecture and costumes, he had, of course, no photograph, no drawing, no portable painting, no bas-relief from Roman ruins; these had not yet been brought to England and no public museums existed in the Eternal City. His Rome was almost certainly the Rome of 1580–90; his Romans were the citizens of the Papal realm; the Senators he saw were the magistrates and civil servants of the Holy Roman rather than the Imperial Roman Empire. This was the vision which we attempted to present to the American public.

"In the first Stratford production, the Senators wore magnificent robes of burgundy velvet; they resembled the crowds in the Raphael frescoes in the Vatican. . . . As for scenery or architecture, the stage was set with the background of a great flight of steps which might have been the Capitoline steps or the stairs to a shrine. In front of this, on two shifting stages which rolled in and out, were the abstracted rooms of Caesar's palace and Brutus' house. They were the sort of cut-through rooms seen in Italian paintings, in which the three walls of a house represent the whole building. Suggestions of the city, in which steps and houses were set, extended in painted scenery well into the auditorium (covering the side galleries outside the proscenium) so that Rome seemed to encompass the audience."

This last device was not successful; by opening night it had been discarded. Lack of time and money had inhibited the full execution of a concept which was, at best, graphic and literary rather than theatrical. Dramatically, the architectural scenery proved rigid and limiting; visually, the painted stonework clashed fatally with the natural wood of the theatre's interior.

The Tempest was conceived as a masque, in the Inigo Jones or Campion manner, centering around the jagged, translucent coral mass of Prospero's enchanted isle. Here again there seemed to be no clear, creative collaboration between director and designer. Once again there were last-minute problems of time and money, so that between the conception and the execution scales were altered; scenery designed to be three-dimensional was rendered as flat and many of the magic effects were lost.

The Tempest, a rehearsal

The Tempest, the shipwreck
Designed by HORACE ARMISTEAD

Indeed, it was not until the third, the "student," production of *Much Ado about Nothing* that the Festival stage seemed to find itself in relation to its audience. The Academy's director, John Burrell, himself a designer and director with the Old Vic in its palmiest days, enjoyed one priceless advantage: having witnessed the first two productions, he and his designer, Robert Fletcher, were able to prepare their comedy with the full knowledge and direct experience of the Festival stage. His single set and much of his stage action were limited to an area almost entirely below the curtain line. For the first and only time good use was made of the balconies outside the proscenium. The result

Much Ado about Nothing (August 1955), the "student" production, directed by JOHN BURRELL, scenery and costumes designed by ROBERT FLETCHER

47

was a modest but satisfying production and an illustration of the one consistent tendency which has pervaded all changes and transformations in the Festival stage: a constant movement of the playing area *downstage toward the audience.* It is no accident that, of its twelve productions, it was *Julius Caesar,* the first, that was set the farthest upstage, and the twelfth, *The Winter's Tale,* which played more of its vital action farther downstage than any of its predecessors.

1956: THE NEW LOOK

THE 1956 Festival season presented two major challenges to its newly appointed directors— John Houseman and Jack Landau. Both related to the general problems of classical repertory and to the special problems of the Festival and its stage. On the one hand, a company of actors must be formed with some degree of cohesion and some hope of continuity; on the other, the stage must be adapted to provide them with a suitable platform on

PLAN OF THE STAGE — 1955–1956
BLACK: Structural Line of Proscenium and Auditorium Walls
LIGHT GRAY: Apron Line — *1955*
WHITE: Festival Stage — *1956* (platforms, steps and ramps added to original stage structure and reconstructed auditorium walls)
BROKEN LINES: Masking System — "Slats"

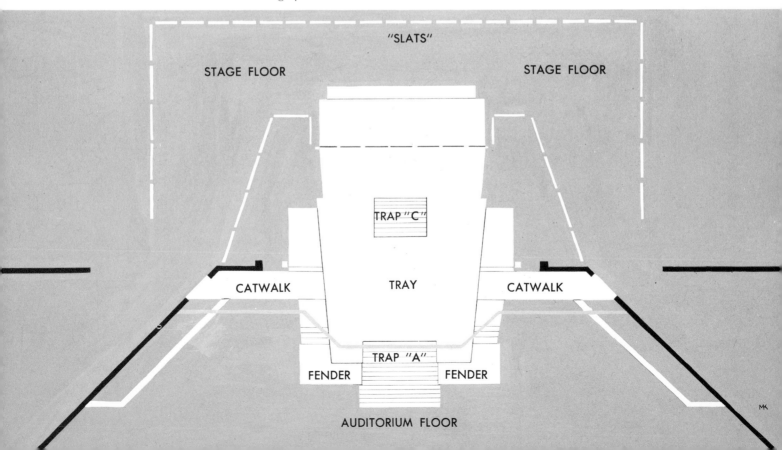

which to perform whichever of Shakespeare's plays— tragical, comical, pastoral, historical— came to be chosen for the season's repertory.

Just as it is impossible in one sweep to recruit a company that is all things to all plays, so it is impossible to devise a stage which will be all things to all productions. The three plays selected for the second Festival season had the widest possible range: the rigorous archaism of *King John;* the bittersweet, almost perverse sophistication of *Measure for Measure;* the simple, lusty mountebank mood of *The Taming of the Shrew.* For the production of these three so widely different theatre pieces, a new and flexible stage had to be devised within the handsome, existing structure of the Festival theatre— one on which it was hoped to combine the blunt immediacy of the Elizabethan platform stage with the visual variety that lies within the depths of a dramatically lighted proscenium arch. This was no unit set, but a functional stage-form within which each production must be free to develop its own individual quality— its size and shape and color— and, above all, its own particular style, through which it could most clearly and directly communicate its quality to a contemporary American audience.

This was the hope— and, in pursuit of it, many trips were made to Stratford during the spring of 1956. Rouben Ter-Arutunian (the designer chosen for the season), Jean Rosenthal, Lincoln Kirstein, together with the two directors and an harassed stage manager, shuffled chairs, planks and sticks of wood across the stage, over the existing apron and the gaping orchestra pit; they sat in remote corners of the balcony, checking sight lines as a fire bucket or a small bag of nails, representing Faulconbridge or Isabella, began a journey around the edges of the imaginary new stage. John Houseman, extending experiments he had begun in earlier productions of *King Lear* and *Coriolanus,* conceived of the new stage floor as a large raked platform of diminishing width, beginning far upstage and projecting as deep into the audience as the sight lines would allow. Jack Landau was thinking of a platform where "the elements of scenery became color and texture, light and form, costume, props, and, most important, the moving figure of the actor."

Ter-Arutunian designed this platform and its appendages and approaches as a "floating" architectural unit cantilevered or

The directors *(1956-1958)*

ROUBEN TER-ARUTUNIAN

JEAN ROSENTHAL

49

The open platform — with its traps and catwalks; ramps and counter-ramps seemed bewildering at first (in the background, the first strip of slats)

supported on thin, set-back, almost invisible legs. At one stroke he solved the double problem of closing in the stage and losing the hard frame of the proscenium arch which had set up such an insuperable barrier between the audience and the actor. On either side of the stage two huge pillars, each a foot square (not unlike the "posts" of the Elizabethan theatre), built of the same teakwood as the interior of the building, were set in the stage floor, running the full height of the proscenium arch (29 ft. 6 in.). This had the advantage of adding two more "accesses" to the platform; for it was one of the requirements of the new stage that functionally (though not visually) it should resemble the stage of Shakespeare's day— with its total absence of scene changes, its great variety of playing areas and its multiplicity of exits and entrances. On the new Festival stage there were eighteen of them, including six entrances from the sides, four upstage, steps set at various angles, ramps, counter-ramps and traps. As part of the move to unify the stage and the auditorium, the Elizabethan "boxes" on either side of the proscenium disappeared under sets of vertical louvers which served as masking for the banks of side lights required by the new downstage area.

For such a large, open area, "masking" becomes a vexing problem. To enclose such an aggressively modern architectural form, velour curtains were excluded; so was the tedious expanse of the familiar cyclorama. To harmonize with the strong, natural-wood texture of the auditorium, it was felt that the side and rear walls of the stage must also be of wood; but the weight and mass of wooden construction made this impracticable. The problem was finally solved by hanging wooden strips, in double layers, around the stage in a solid-seeming wall, which, in fact, allowed more than the usual passageroom for lights and actors. These were made up of strips of crating painted silvery brown, of random widths varying from four to seven inches, all equally spaced, one inch apart, and mounted on two parallel lines of heavy canvas tape. Sixty-three such sections were assembled (amounting to 10,000 square feet of wood), each capable of moving separately up and down with a blindlike motion.

Some of these ideas for the new stage were developed on the drawing board; most of them underwent growth and change as the result of experiments and observations on the stage itself. In the course of work a convenient terminology was evolved among the collaborators. The huge central ramped platform was re-

In the basement, the wardrobe mistress (LILLIAS NOREL)

"Slats" — 63 sections, 10,000 feet.
A dress rehearsal of *King John,*
final scene

Trap "A" — waiting for an entrance   "The Walls of Angiers" — the citizens look down

ferred to as the "tray" or "rake." The side approaches were known as the "cat walk." Its extreme downstage extensions became the "fenders." The slatted walls were referred to as "skins," "slats," "Venetian blinds," "orange crates" and other terms of endearment. A large two-storied platform at the upstage end of the "tray" bore the noble name of "Angiers" from the beleaguered town whose battlements it first represented. Each of the three stage traps (each with its own special machinery developed by Al Johnson, the Festival's first carpenter) had its own individual appelation. The main one, opening out of the extreme downstage end of the raked platform, was known as "Trap A." Because it operates on the principle of a garage door, opening and closing in absolute silence, its installation involved blasting three feet of concrete from the auditorium floor and the loss of two rows of seats. But it was worth it, for "Trap A" has become the Festival stage's busiest thoroughfare. Farther upstage, two additional traps were planned— "B" and "C." "B" ran into structural entanglements with the steel beams supporting the building and was eliminated. "C," its sliding top opening about six feet upstage of the curtain line, marks the normal upstage limit of the playing area. It has served such varied uses as a secret issue for murderers, a death cell for condemned prisoners, Ophelia's grave, Oberon's private entrance into the magic wood, and the springboard for "Time's" incongruous leap across the centuries in *The Winter's Tale*.

Over the years, these scenic forms and devices have become familiar and characteristic elements of the Festival's productions; but when the company arrived in Stratford in the first week of

52

June 1956 to begin technical and dress rehearsals for the second Festival season, they found them strange and disturbing.

For four weeks the company had been rehearsing in New York under the joint direction of Houseman and Landau, on a concrete warehouse floor, marked with multicolored tape to indicate the dimensions and levels of the new stage. Now, as they tripped and clambered up and down the still-unpainted forms and angles of this bare and open platform, they found cause to doubt their directors' wisdom, if not their sanity.

The two plays in which they were to open "back to back," on successive nights, had only one thing in common— their unfamiliarity to the audience. Of all Shakespeare's plays, it is doubtful if two have ever been more unlike— in theme, in tone, in period, in acting and production styles— than *King John* and *Measure for Measure* as produced at the Festival. *King John* is a crude and savage historical tragedy; characters move through a grim world of castles, walled towns, camps, battlefields, sea coasts and dungeons to their tragic climax in an orchard, where the king finally dies in agony to the muffled booming of an abbey bell. All these were indicated in the Festival production by light-changes on a stage empty save for an occasional massive throne or stool. Changes of place and form were effected by the rise and fall of the wooden walls, while the "traps" opened and closed to the accompaniment of Virgil Thomson's somber, military fanfares, to give the sense of secret stairs, sea shores and the foul mouths of dungeons. Ter-Arutunian's costumes were oversized— epic in bulk and weight. (At the dress parade three nobles and seven soldiers keeled over. After hundreds of pounds of cotton stuffing were removed and burned and holes punched in helmets and rubber boots, the fainting rate fell to about one a week.) All this gave the production a kind of rugged splendor, but served

JOHN EMERY as King John

Costume design: Coronation robes

KENDALL CLARK as the Papal Legate

"Epic in bulk" — costumes by ROUBEN TER-ARUTUNIAN

Measure for Measure:
Vienna — a street

The Provost, Morris Carnovsky; Claudio, Donald Harron; Lucio, Norman Lloyd; Juliet, Jacqueline Brookes; Officers, Rod Colbin and Mitchell Agruss

to accentuate its stiff and formal character. *King John* was received with respect but without any of the enthusiasm that greeted the following night's performance of *Measure for Measure,* which was unquestionably aided by the violent contrast not only in the texts of the two plays but also in their production styles.

Measure for Measure is one of Shakespeare's "difficult" plays — a "dark" comedy about which there is little critical agreement. The Festival directors, having chosen to play it lightly, for irony rather than terror, had laid it not in fifteenth- but in nineteenth-century Vienna. The costumes (again Ter-Arutunian's) ranged from the bright uniforms, capes and plumes of Hapsburg operetta to the tawdry underworld of *The Threepenny Opera.* Pompey was bowler-hatted with a red-and-white-striped silk shirt; the Duke departed the capital complete with hunting stick, dog and caged bird, in a pelisse and hat of Tyrolian green; Angelo, out of office, wore a Prince Albert— in office, his costume was modeled after a photograph of Jean Cocteau the day he was admitted to the French Academy.

Overnight the stage, too, had lost some of its medieval severity. The ducal palace boasted a red carpet, running the full depth of the raked stage, which was rolled up, after the Duke's

Mistress Overdone, Tomi Romer; Pompey, Hiram Sherman

Measure for Measure
finale!

exit, by two footmen in scarlet liveries. Overhead, across its entire width, a vast crimson, gold-fringed swag of damask hung high above a pair of crystal chandeliers. Vienna's red-light district had posters in the Lautrec manner and echoed to the sounds of a mechanical piano playing the current waltz hit, "Take, Oh, Take Those Lips Away!" (music by Virgil Thomson). Angelo's first encounter with Isabella took place across the green baize of his official table, the second in the small circle of light bounded by a Biedermeier bentwood sofa and one straight-backed chair. The jail was timeless— a maze of bars and dungeons, lighted to suggest a small-scale Piranesi prison. Ragozine's head was delivered to the surrogate in a fine leather hat box of the period. Finally, to celebrate the Duke's return and Angelo's downfall, the gates of the city were coiffed with a baroque sunburst, orange and white flags and strings of colored lanterns.

Measure for Measure proved to be the Festival's first unqualified critical and popular success. Brooks Atkinson, in *The New York Times*, found it "a particularly winning piece of theatre— lightly devised, ingeniously staged, played lightly . . . it deserves a hundred and one performances in the inviting theatre on the Housatonic." "Utterly captivating," wrote John

The Duke, ARNOLD MOSS; Angelo,
KENDALL CLARK (*New York, 1957*)

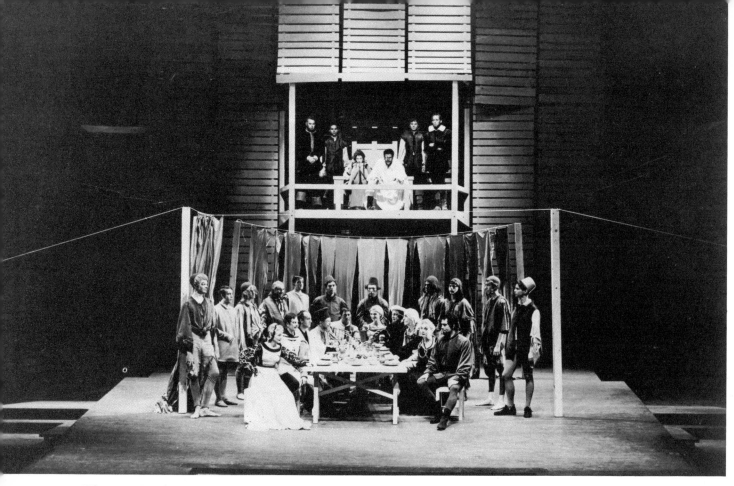

The Taming of the Shrew:
Christopher Sly (MIKE KELLIN)
and Page (SUSAN LLOYD) watch
the wedding feast. Costumes by
DOROTHY JEAKINS

Kate, NINA FOCH, and the Widow,
PAMELA SAUNDERS

Chapman of the *Daily News,* "a lovely rollicking farce"— and he urged his readers to "hurry as fast as possible up the Merritt Parkway to see it."

Later in the season, a modest but lively production of *The Taming of the Shrew* was put on. As directed by Norman Lloyd, it presented some stimulating acting problems to the company. Scenically, it was the season's simplest production. For the "Induction" severe black and white Elizabethan fashions were used; for the traveling players, Dorothy Jeakins designed some Italianate costumes that were athletic yet bright and full of character. Use of the stage's mechanical resources was deliberately avoided. The "A trap" was constantly open and all the panels were kept lowered throughout the action to form the three wooden walls of a courtyard. On a small balcony jutting out from the back wall Christopher Sly had his bed and watched the traveling actors as they arrived and rigged the posts and stained, ragged curtains of their own small, improvised stage. Irwin Bazelon's gay circus music enhanced this mountebank mood, and the summer audience seemed delighted with it.

During August *Shrew* and *Measure* together started to ring up the Festival's first substantial weekly receipts and to attract growing numbers of the general public, many of whom had never before seen one of Shakespeare's plays professionally performed.

Yet it was with *King John* and *Measure for Measure,* presented by the same company, on the same stage, on successive nights, that the Festival definitely established its character as a serious theatrical venture. It is of these two productions that Robert Hatch was writing in *The Nation* when he made his detailed and perceptive analysis of the new stage and its dramatic possibilities:

"The second summer at Stratford, Connecticut, will be remembered as the season when the American Shakespeare Festival learned to use its remarkable theatre. . . . The present setting is entirely simple and completely encompassing. The raked floor of the stage extends at least as far forward of the proscenium as there is depth behind it. There is a broad, easy stair from below stage at the front of the apron and at stage center a trap, also large and of easy access, down which a whole troop can on occasion plunge at full tilt. The three sides of the stage back of the proscenium are framed to immense height and width by horizontal slats of neutral wood hung in a large number of panels and in two or more ranks deep. These panels can be raised or lowered individually in almost numberless combinations to suggest gates, doors, chambers, passageways of whatever importance; segments high in them can be swung up to evoke battlements or the windows of a ribald house— in the present instance; the allusive possibilities are infinite. Light can come from behind the slats, diffused; it can hit against them or glance across them, and the wood offers a warm or forbidding surface as the color and quality of the light determine. . . . The walls can seem solid barriers or yielding curtains; they can be dappled with shadow as is the world outdoors. Changes of scene take place as it were instantaneously and the swift geometry of the evolutions contributes to the dramatic urgency. Though these slatted walls are tall and frame a huge space, they do not give the eye any units for measurement, and they offer a background against which the actors, when it is useful, can appear in stereoscopic perspective. The result is that the performers are close without being intimate; they stand large and can move with large, carrying gestures. It is a marvelously sensitive setting but so empty that whatever moves onto it is instantly endowed with great moment."

Not everyone shared Mr. Hatch's aesthetic enthusiasm. Some of the Festival's more conservative patrons found the stage bare and arid and yearned for the representational values of the past. Others found the "slats" and their up-and-down movements monotonous; there were the inevitable jokes about cigar boxes and Venetian blinds. Yet it was clear by now that from a practical as well as creative point of view, the new Festival stage had proved itself an essential and invaluable element in establishing not only the artistic but also the commercial and popular identity of the Festival.

During the winter two of the summer productions, *Measure for Measure* and *The Taming of the Shrew*, were presented for a limited run at the Phoenix Theatre in New York. For this engagement a portable and simplified version of the Festival stage was built, in which some of the "floating" effect was lost and the use of traps and ramps somewhat restricted, but the essential quality of the Festival stage was retained. This same stage was used in a third production, *The Duchess of Malfi*. Presented by the Phoenix Theatre in association with John Houseman, it was performed by members of the Festival Company and directed by Jack Landau. Two steep flights of open stairs leading to an upper gallery and clouds of heavy-fringed, black velour curtains evoked the surrealist world of John Webster's Elizabethan nightmare. Two of these elements— steps and gallery— were to be used in various forms in subsequent Festival productions.

1957: THE NEXT STEP

As preparations began for the new season, the production staff considered certain additions to the Stratford stage. Some were elements which formed part of the designer's original conception but had not, through pressure of time and money, been included in the 1956 productions. These were now re-examined in the light of the previous season's experience, and readjusted to meet the specific requirements of the plays which had been announced for 1957— *Othello, The Merchant of Venice, Much Ado about Nothing*.

In all these considerations, the basic aesthetic intention remained— to retain the identity of the Festival stage without

The switchboard — stage right   Thunder and wind — stage left

allowing it to become monotonous; to gain added speed and variety without loss of simplicity or strength.

After much debate a "machine" was devised which would move scenery and furniture (and even actors) up and down stage without human intervention and which would, at the same time, solve the spatial problem of the "Inner Stage" which the Festival's version of Shakespeare's space-stage had not yet fully accomplished. Three winch-operated platforms on broad, heavy rollers were installed on the "tray"— one main central platform (12 ft. wide and 8 ft. deep) flanked by two lesser (4 ft.) platforms on either side. These moved in silence, drawn by fine wire cables, on sunken fiber tracks which seemed, if they were at all apparent, like elegant vertical lines on the raked wooden floor

The winch for the moving platform — basement

All these are controlled by

the Stage Manager, BERNARD GERSTEN

59

Othello, the Council Chamber

Othello, Act I

of the stage. Winch gears and cores had been ground especially, and these were mounted on a shoemaker's form set in the basement outside the dressing-room area, directly under the upstage end of the platform.

With this new machinery, rapid and striking transformations could be effected in full sight of the audience. The council chamber in the first act of *Othello* (with its heavy oak table, tall chairs, and green-and-gold canopy overhead) became the exterior of the fort in Cyprus with no more delay than it took to make the light change from the murk of the Doge's palace to the stormy brilliance of the Mediterranean sky. The council table, on the central "machine," receded, while the gates of Cyprus, mounted on the side machines (complete with woven portcullis and solid wooden buttresses), moved down— the one seeming to swallow up the other. The transformation was made even more impressive by the simultaneous, silent opening of the "A trap," through which Cypriot soldiers began to emerge while lights and scenery were still in motion.

Equivalent transformations were accomplished in *The Merchant of Venice.* For its continuous, rapid alternation of scenes, from the Rialto to Belmont to Shylock's house and back again, architectural pieces were devised for the "machines" which moved under the slim, golden bridge that spanned the entire stage as a constant reminder of Venice.

Though both plays were produced in "period" and both made use of the same mechanical elements, *Othello* and *The Merchant* were quite different in mood and appearance. The Moor's tragedy was staged in the austere *King John* mode, using the full area of the "rake" except for the final scene of Desdemona's death, when a lustrous silk-canopied bed occupied the center of the stage. Costumes were formal, but without the massive excesses of *King John*. Every attempt was made to point up the contrast between the somber opulence of Venice and the sun-drenched, sea-girt, military world of Cyprus. Here rope, leather, tenting and fishnet, hung against the texture of the stage's permanent wooden lattices, were the materials of the background and decoration.

The Merchant of Venice, with Katharine Hepburn for its star, was the Festival's most decorative and elaborate production. Across its delicate golden bridge, under its canopies of flowered ribbon, through its soaring baroque arches, moved Motley's theatrical figures in velvets and silks. Only Morris Carnovsky's Shylock ranged dark and alien through this elegant, festive world.

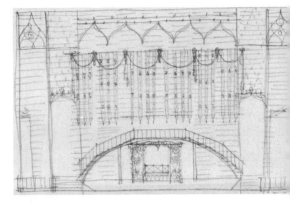

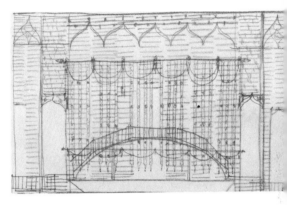

The Merchant of Venice: Belmont
Katharine Hepburn as Portia; Lois Nettleton as Nerissa

[*Left*]
"*Hath not a Jew eyes?*"

[*Above*]
A rehearsal: the Trial Scene, MORRIS CARNOVSKY as Shylock

[*Below left*]
PORTIA: "*Come, Nerissa . . . While we shut the gates upon one wooer, another knocks at the door.*"

[*Below right*]
A fitting: Miss Hepburn with "MOTLEY" (ELIZABETH MONTGOMERY), designer

Much Ado about Nothing opened late in July and came to be known as the "Rio Grande" or "Texas" production of Shakespeare's comedy. The locale and period were selected for reasons which the directors felt to be theatrically and textually valid. First, it seemed undesirable to present a third consecutive production against an Italian Renaissance background. Further, it seemed necessary to find a world within which the trivial border affray of the play's opening and the "great house" and "house party" atmosphere of the whole piece could be presented comprehensibly to an American audience. (Other requirements were that it take place within a Catholic society, that its costumes be romantic, and that the local police force be familiarly corrupt

Much Ado about Nothing (Texas style)

The wedding morning — inside . . .   . . . and outside

and comical.) The production idea was born when Katharine Hepburn presented the Festival's directors with an illustrated history of the King Ranch in southern Texas. The following week Rouben Ter-Arutunian set to work on scenery and costumes and Virgil Thomson began his research into the border and barrelhouse folk music of the mid-nineteenth century.

Although the production of *Much Ado* seemed to mark a retreat from the original concept of the Festival stage, it provided certain new ideas. Its set— a solid two-story hacienda with an overhanging red-tiled roof— related to the familiar wooden walls of the Festival stage by the fact that it was entirely built of the same slats, surfaced in stucco and painted white. No house curtain was used. In its place two lateral sections of wall— seven feet high, also built of stucco slats, and pushed on telescoping tracks by barefoot, straw-hatted peons— occupied the downstage width of the stage. In the middle, mounted on the center machine, were the gates of Leonato's house. This permitted another striking

63

The Great House

Dogberry

Don Pedro

Scenery and costumes
by ROUBEN TER-ARUTUNIAN

transformation. As Don Pedro's army marched upstage through them to the accompaniment of a brisk, martial air, the gates receded and the walls opened, revealing the courtyard of the "great house," its steps and galleries crowded with cheering, flower-tossing ladies. When the army reappeared seconds later to accept this rousing welcome, it was through the same gates— but now from the rear, coming from the opposite direction, marching downstage. In other words, the whole stage had been turned inside out before the audience's eyes. (This combined use of the lateral wall and the "machine" was to lead to further development in the Festival stage.)

It was this production of *Much Ado,* starring Katharine Hepburn and Alfred Drake, which the Festival sent out in the following winter and spring on a tour of six major Eastern cities. With minor structural modifications the identical set was used, except that (for reasons of space and economy in transportation) the raked tray and winch were eliminated for the "road," and the platforms, with their scenery and furniture, were moved manually by the peons of Leonato's estate.

Nineteen fifty-seven was an encouraging year for the American Shakespeare Festival. With every production the company was becoming more cohesive and developing its own character and style of classical acting. Critically, the Festival had attained unquestioned parity with the other two Stratfords. With attendance more than double that of the first year, its summer season was now almost self-supporting. The tour of *Much Ado,* though hurriedly undertaken, just about broke even financially, and introduced the American Shakespeare Festival Company in such important audience centers as Philadelphia, Detroit, Cleveland, St. Louis, Washington and Boston to general critical and editorial acclaim.

As the directors began to plan for their next season, however, they were faced with the disturbing realization that their production costs showed a steady rise from year to year, particularly in scenic construction and costumes. The latter could be explained by the heavy requirements of the three plays selected for 1957, but the increased cost of scenery gave rise to serious thoughts about the future development of the Festival stage.

The new mechanical additions had proved themselves beyond any doubt. The disturbing thing was that, with all these new aids and conveniences, the weight and amount of scenery on the stage were constantly growing and with them the crew required to work the shows and to make the daily, and sometimes twice-daily, shifts necessary to meet the repertory schedule. Besides, there was a danger even greater than a mere increase in material costs, one that threatened the whole basic concept of the Festival stage. In 1956 there had been a minimum of scenery; in 1957 there seemed to be a maximum. Mass was being substituted for function. The fact that a second-story window unit had to be built for *Othello,* a bridge for *The Merchant of Venice* and a gallery for *Much Ado about Nothing,* all situated in exactly the same place, indicated that the Festival's permanent stage was not yet completely realized.

1958: FOLLOWING STEPS

THIS WAS the background against which the plans for the fourth Festival season were worked out. Rouben Ter-Arutunian was in Europe and David Hays took his place as set designer; the costumes for *Hamlet, A Midsummer Night's Dream* and *The Winter's Tale* were assigned respectively to Alvin Colt, Thea Neu and Dorothy Jeakins.

For the stage, the plans included a fixed but flexible upstage gallery, which would supply all future sets with a movable inner and a permanent upper stage. This was a simple platform (seven feet high and six feet deep) supported on solid wooden legs spaced to give passage to the three sections of the "machine." This structure, the equivalent of what the scholars call the "Inner Above" of the Elizabethan stage, became known as the "Gallery." It spanned the entire stage at approximately the same position as that occupied the previous year by the gallery of *Much Ado* and the bridge of *The Merchant.* Exits to the side and back were provided, and, at either end, two optional sections eight feet long, running downstage, at right angles to it. Good use was made of this "gallery" in *Hamlet* and *A Midsummer Night's Dream.* Here were the upper reaches of the battlements— the ghost's territory. Here, in *Dream,* was the minstrel gallery as well as the treetop aerie of Oberon and Titania.

The gain in intimacy and flexibility achieved through the

HAMLET

Designs by David Hays

use of the telescoping walls in the 1957 production of *Much Ado* led to the invention of the "Colonnade." This is best described as a long, narrow platform on legs approximately eight feet high whose two equal sections completely fill the proscenium when they are in a closed position; in this position they also meet the downstage extensions of the "gallery." This provided— in *Hamlet*, for example— a courtyard above and around which the Swiss guard could keep their quiet watch and along whose upper levels Hamlet would walk, silent and alone. On its lower level, the colonnade played an important part in Ophelia's life. It is here that she met Hamlet for the "Nunnery Scene" and here that she appeared, with flowers, on her way to watery death.

In the main, *Hamlet* continued the Festival's austere tradition of *King John* and *Othello*. The score by Virgil Thomson included parts for two open trumpets, a recorder, two field drums and a bagpipe. It was costumed in the Holbein manner and played on a stage that was almost entirely free of props and whose scenery, in addition to the new "gallery" and "colonnade," consisted of variations in the positions of three sets of high wooden, open stairs, mounted on the machines and capable of individual movement. This gave speed and variety to the action of what was an unusually full version of the text. Some found the steps obtrusive and the whole stage "suggestive of a gymnasium," but the Canadian critic Herbert Whittaker thought it was "a remarkable one. Pretending to openness and the plainness of wood, adhering to its devotion to the blinds of Venice, it is actually a most subtle and ingenious platform. The major elements of this particular production are a grandstand of steps which moves majestically forward and back and a bridge which splits asunder, then joins again to provide an upper stage. Backing these two major structures are the familiar, high-reaching, slatted walls which are translucent and almost transparent in the brilliance of Jean Rosenthal's lighting."

By way of contrast, *A Midsummer Night's Dream* was mounted in festive Elizabethan manner. A key to the production style was the notion of the play as a masque performed on the occasion of some country nobleman's wedding. Theseus' palace became a Tudor hall complete with tapestry, choir screen and courtly music (composed by Marc Blitzstein and sung by counter-tenor Russell Oberlin). For the transformation into the forest, sections of the gilded wooden screen detached themselves,

INGA SWENSON as Ophelia,
FRITZ WEAVER as Hamlet

JUNE HAVOC as Titania,
RICHARD WARING as Oberon

67

A Midsummer Night's Dream   The Palace   The Forest

traveled downstage on the "machines" and formed mobile bowers
through which human beings and fairy folk pursued each other,
while the forest itself was indicated by a tapestry (in Gobelin
style) which stretched and rose till it became a vast, luminous
background of blue-green and gold. All the characters, the human beings (the nobles with their servants, minstrels, the middle-
class lovers, the rude mechanicals) as well as the fairies (Titania
with her sprightly train, Oberon with his guard of treemen and
Puck as a cross between forest faun and a mischievous adolescent
in an Eton jacket) were essentially and unmistakably English.

Each season the Festival's third production seems to possess
some special quality of its own. *The Winter's Tale* was no excep-
tion. It was the simplest, yet perhaps the most sophisticated production to be mounted on the Festival stage. It proved a val-

68

uable example of what can be achieved with an imaginative production idea, given time to mature, and executed with care, economy and style.

The Winter's Tale is a perplexing play, broken into two parts which, on the surface, fail to match or cohere. For this reason it was essential to find a style, both of acting and of direction, that would encompass its extreme changes of mood— one sufficiently formal to give the characters their legendary quality, yet not so remote from life as to negate the human emotions they undergo. A solution for this blend of ritual and reality was suggested by the ancient, semi-political, semi-religious symbols of the Mediterranean Tarot card pack.

This idea was Lincoln Kirstein's and it evoked an immediate response in Dorothy Jeakins' imaginative costume designs. The opposing emblems of Sun and Moon, the casual contrasts and the recurrent symbols of Sword, Cup, Sheaf and Club gave a simple and very special aspect to the production which David Hays carried through in the spare decorations with which he adorned the functional elements of the Festival stage.

In this formal Tarot world of myth, everything became possible: the king's jealous madness, the queen's death and resurrection, the infant Perdita's exposure on the seashore of Bohemia after her abductor had been eaten by a giant polar bear, even Father Time's appearance in the center of the storm under a dripping umbrella in a wrinkled seersucker suit— all these seemed poetically and dramatically credible.

With this production, the Festival stage made its own con- 69

The Winter's Tale: "Music, awake her!"

MOON: Sicily

SUN: Bohemia

CUPS: Resurrection

quest of space and proved its capacity for infinite theatrical variety. Moving with complete freedom, the action alternated between scenes staged in deliberately restricted areas and those in which the dimension of the stage space was used to its full depth and height— sixty thousand cubic feet of electrically luminous gloom surrounding a single human figure and some fluttering strips of China silk became the storm that separates the two halves of the play.

As in all Festival productions, light was the unifying element. The electrical setup which allows great variety within each production as well as total change of mood and style, from play to play, was the original creation of Jean Rosenthal. She was joined in 1957 by Tharon Musser, who is credited with the lighting of *Much Ado about Nothing* and *A Midsummer Night's Dream*.

The Festival stage is the continuing work of many people. Within four years it has become a familiar theatrical form. It has been directly imitated. Echoes and reflections of it can be seen in the design of many recent Broadway and Off-Broadway productions. This is a happy kind of recognition. But its true measure of success lies in its theatricality and flexibility. It has allowed for endless reinvestigation and adaptation; it has placed no restrictions on the designers, the directors or the actors who have played upon it. Each of these has found it a liberating and rewarding world in which to create.

· III ·
The Acting Company
1955-1958

A THEATRE is something besides a piece of real estate; it is more than an address or a hall available to anyone with the rent in his pocket. A theatre is a small universe in which the stage, the auditorium and its surroundings, the artistic program and the business policy, the actors, the directors, the technicians and, last but not least, the audience all combine to form a living and growing whole.

Historically, the titles "Old Vic," "Moscow Art Theatre," "Comédie Française" refer no less to the acting members of these famous institutions than to the buildings in which they perform. So with the American Shakespeare Festival Theatre: the brief histories of the playhouse on the Housatonic and of the acting company which occupies it are virtually inseparable.

This unity was foreseen and desired in the original plans outlined for the Shakespeare Theatre. Although the first Festival season was put together under extreme pressure, the cast assembled (in the summer of 1955) for *Julius Caesar* and *The Tempest,* headed by Raymond Massey and Jack Palance, included a number of the country's best young actors: Christopher Plummer, Fritz Weaver, Earle Hyman, Leora Dana, Hurd Hatfield, Jerry Stiller, Rex Everhart, James Olson, Polly Rowles and Roddy McDowall. But it was not until the next spring that the challenge of forming an American classical acting company could be met with some degree of deliberation.

In preparing for the new season, every element of production— the selection of artistic personnel, the choice of plays and, above all, the recruiting of actors to play in them— was guided by a firm determination to create and develop a continuing and, if possible, permanent theatrical organization around the Festival theatre.

There were those who viewed such a project without enthusiasm. George Jean Nathan, writing of "a place called Stratford, Conn., if you can find it," advised the Festival's founders to "forget all about the local novices and just import some English actors."

The opposite view was put forward in *The New York Times* by John Houseman, the Festival's newly appointed artistic director, who had long expressed and demonstrated his faith in the American actor's ability to perform the classics with a sharpness and a depth of interpretation often missing in actors whose professional lives have been spent entirely in the elocutionary theatre:

"For years American acting was a very honorable branch of the English theatrical tradition. Then, with the rise of a native American drama, there developed an unfortunate but ever-widening chasm between the classic and realistic schools of performance in this country. In the past two generations most of our best young actors have been preoccupied almost exclusively with the inner mechanics of expressing emotions— the much discussed 'method' and its derivatives. The results have been stimulating and far-reaching. Of late, however, even among these actors who are most deeply committed to the subjective systems, there has been a growing preoccupation with a more styled and eloquent theatre, a rising impatience with the limitations of the naturalistic stage and a general desire for a freer, more fluid and more lyric communication between stage and auditorium, between the theatrical creation and its audience. In none of the great dramatic periods of the past have these virtues been so clearly marked as in the Elizabethan theatre, and more particularly in the works of William Shakespeare. A season of his plays, if it is to justify its existence, cannot fail to contribute, on both sides of the footlights, to the development of that richer and more dynamic kind of theatre, the desire for which seems to hang so clearly in the American air."

Not all the high hopes of the second Festival season were realized, but enough was achieved to clarify the problems facing ASFTA in the future. Now that the idea of a classical repertory company had moved out of the world of dreams and into the realm of actual accomplishment, it became increasingly clear that means must be found to provide its members with more extensive and continuous activity than was afforded by the brief rehearsal and performance periods of an annual summer season.

IT WAS out of this desire to keep the company alive that a limited winter season was arranged at the Phoenix Theatre in New York. Including rehearsals, this provided the Festival company with three welcome months of additional theatrical activity.

A few weeks after the end of the Phoenix engagement, rehearsals began for the 1957 repertory. Allowing for the normal turnover (which has come to average around 25 per cent from year to year) the company was substantially the same as that of the previous summer. But a new element had been added. First Alfred Drake and then Katharine Hepburn joined the company for the coming Festival season. Both welcomed the Festival's general casting principle— that all its actors appear in no less than two plays in the repertory. But with their participation, certain problems arose which the Festival's directors could neither ignore nor evade. For all the obvious artistic and economic advantages, the presence of so celebrated a stage and film star

73

as Miss Hepburn seemed to present a serious threat to what had become the directors' prime preoccupation—the integration of a permanent acting ensemble. Their doubts proved unfounded. Miss Hepburn's energy and devotion not only contributed greatly to the successful outcome of the season but to the total strength and stability of the company ever since.

It was during the last six weeks of the 1957 season that the sale of standing room became a pleasantly regular habit at the Festival theatre. By Labor Day, for the first time in its history, the Festival was operating in the black. In the brief span of its third season (thirteen weeks extended to fourteen to satisfy the public demand) the company, out of weekly profits, had repaid the full costs of its three productions.

Yet, pleasing and encouraging though it was, the summer's achievement emphasized rather than diminished the gravity of ASFTA's basic problem—the inescapable fact that, no matter how successful a summer season might be, the Festival and its company could never function properly, artistically or economically, or even ultimately survive while operating for only three, or at most four, months of the year.

The winter of 1957–1958 marked a second attempt to struggle out of this dilemma. And here Katharine Hepburn placed ASFTA even more deeply in her debt when she led the Festival company on its first full-scale road tour. Facing a national recession and a series of legendary blizzards, the Festival company visited six major cities and gave them, with *Much Ado about Nothing,* their first sight of the American Shakespeare Festival's acting company and style. Detroit found it *"Theatre magic of the highest kind . . . for these magicians are dedicated people, not only to Shakespeare but to the immortal theatre." "The Bard has found a firm U.S. footing,"* wrote Richard Coe in the Washington *Post. "That our own Stratford—and it is past time that the wealthiest nation in the world had one— is giving excitement to the world's greatest dramatist is an enthralling achievement . . . color, magic and glory suffuse these productions."* Cleveland found in the Festival's performance *"a reason for singing and dancing in the streets. The two stars gleam in this ensemble production and there is lustre everywhere."* The company's appearance in Boston led the *Herald* to ask editorially, *"Are the American people, today, ready to accept Shakespeare?"* and to give its own positive answer: *"The American Shakespeare Theatre says yes and in this hope lies a future for the establishment of our national classic theatre style."*

I₂ THERE was one rueful afterthought to the Festival company's successful tour, it was a regret that only a single play had been performed. Had the summer season's other successful production— *The Merchant of Venice*— been played in repertory with *Much Ado* (though it might have added slightly to the initial expense and labor of the enterprise) it would have been of enormous artistic and financial benefit to the company. There is a vital and revivifying force in repertory that no single production, no matter how glitteringly successful, can provide.

Within six weeks of the tour's end, the Festival company was once again in rehearsal for a new summer season. Except for the departure of its two stars, and the usual half-dozen additions and subtractions elsewhere, the main change in the company was a sharp increase in the number of its members. To satisfy the varied demands of *Hamlet, A Midsummer Night's Dream* and *The Winter's Tale,* the Festival company for the season of 1958 grew to thirty-two, not counting apprentices, extras, stage musicians, elves and dogs. The directors took this opportunity to contract a number of actors and actresses whom they had long wished to bring into the company. The added financial burden was fortunately absorbed by the overwhelming popular success which the 1958 Festival season enjoyed from the first preview to the closing performance of its fourteen-week season. Numerically, there was a further rise in attendance of about twenty per cent over the previous season. This encouraged the belief that, in its first four years, The American Shakespeare Festival Theatre had achieved a real degree of stability and continuity.

No less satisfying was the realization that with this season's last performance, members of the acting company had been steadily employed for twenty out of the past twenty- seven months. During this time they had rehearsed and appeared (between eighteen and ninety-three times apiece) in ten full-sized classical productions. Under the conditions currently prevailing in the American theatre, this record was unique and astonishing.

75

KEY TO ABBREVIATIONS

JC – JULIUS CAESAR (1955)

T – THE TEMPEST (1955)

KJ – KING JOHN (1956)

MM – MEASURE FOR MEASURE (1956)

TS – THE TAMING OF THE SHREW (1956)

MM-Ph – MEASURE FOR MEASURE at the Phoenix Theatre, New York (1957)

TS-Ph – THE TAMING OF THE SHREW at the Phoenix Theatre, New York (1957)

O – OTHELLO (1957)

MOV – THE MERCHANT OF VENICE (1957)

MA – MUCH ADO ABOUT NOTHING (1957)

MA-tour – MUCH ADO ABOUT NOTHING tour (1958)

H – HAMLET (1958)

MND – A MIDSUMMER NIGHT'S DREAM (1958)

WT – THE WINTER'S TALE (1958)

AGRUSS, MITCHELL: Prince Henry (**KJ**), 1st Gentleman (**MM**), Tranio (**TS**), 1st Gentleman (**MM-Ph**), Tranio (**TS-Ph**), Cypriot Servant (**O**), Conrade (**MA**), Conrade (**MA-tour**), Marcellus and Poisoner (**H**), Angelo (**WT**).

ASHWORTH, TUCKER: 2nd Gentleman (**MM-Ph**), Huntsman (**TS-Ph**).

BAKER, VIRGINIA: Juno (**T**).

BARRIE, BARBARA: Player Queen (**H**), Hermia (**MND**), Dorcas (**WT**).

BATES, RONALD: Stage Manager (**KJ**), (**MM**), (**TS**), (**MM-Ph**), (**TS-Ph**), (**O**), (**MOV**), (**MA**).

BELL, STANLEY: Escalus (**MM**), A Lord (**TS**), Duke of Venice (**O**), Prince of Arragon (**MOV**), Don Pedro (**MA**), Don Pedro (**MA-tour**).

BITTNER, JACK: Montano (**O**), Tubal (**MOV**), Borachio (**MA**), Borachio (**MA-tour**), Ghost (**H**), Theseus (**MND**), Time and 1st Gentleman (**WT**).

BLOFSON, RICHARD: Stage Manager (**MA-tour**), (**H**), (**MND**), (**WT**).

BORDON, MICHAEL: Balthazar (**MA-tour**).

BOURNEUF, PHILIP: Gremio (**TS-Ph**).

BROOKES, JACQUELINE: Blanche (**KJ**), Juliet (**MM**), Juliet (**MM-Ph**), Desdemona (**O**), Ursula (**MA**), Ursula (**MA-tour**).

CAHILL, JAMES: Nathaniel (**TS-Ph**), 2nd Watchman (**MA-tour**).

CANNON, JACK: Volumnius and Cinna (**JC**).

CARNOVSKY, MORRIS: Earl of Salisbury (**KJ**), Provost (**MM**), Grumio (**TS**), Provost (**MM-Ph**), Grumio (**TS-Ph**), Shylock (**MOV**), Antonio (**MA**), Claudius (**H**), Quince (**MND**).

CHANDLER, JOAN: Miranda (**T**).

CLARK, KENDALL: Cardinal Pandulph (**KJ**), Hortensio (**TS**), Hortensio (**TS-Ph**), Gratiano (**O**), Solanio (**MOV**), Friar Francis (**MA**).

COLBIN, ROD: Executioner (**KJ**), 2nd Gentleman (**MM**), Adam (**TS**), Curtis (**TS-Ph**).

COLICOS, JOHN: Lodovico (**O**), Gratiano (**MOV**), Leonato (**MA**), Leonato (**MA-tour**), Laertes (**H**), Lysander (**MND**), Leontes (**WT**).

COTTRELL, WILLIAM: Robert Faulconbridge (**KJ**), Elbow (**MM**), Tailor (**TS**), Abhorson (**MM-Ph**), Huntsman and Tailor (**TS-Ph**), 1st Senator (**O**), Old Gobbo (**MOV**), 2nd Watchman (**MA**), 1st Watchman (**MA-tour**).

DANA, LEORA: Portia (**JC**), Ceres (**T**).

DARDEN, SEVERN: Voltemand (**H**), Snug (**MND**), Officer and 2nd Gentleman (**WT**).

DEERING, OLIVE: Bianca (**O**).

DEUTSCH, BENITA: Servant (**MA-tour**).

DONAT, PETER: Metellus Cimber and Lucilius (**JC**).

DORONNE, DINA: Jessica (**MOV**), Hero (**MA-tour**).

DRAKE, ALFRED: Iago (**O**), Benedick (**MA**), Benedick (**MA-tour**).

DUNNOCK, MILDRED: Constance (**KJ**).

DURHAM, RICHARD: Archduke of Austria (**KJ**), Justice (**MM**).

EASTON, RICHARD: Claudio (**MM-Ph**), Lucentio (**TS-Ph**), Roderigo (**O**), Lancelot Gobbo (**MOV**), Claudio (**MA**), Claudio (**MA-tour**), Osric (**H**), Puck (**MND**), Florizel (**WT**).

EDMONDS, LOUIS: A Lord (**TS-Ph**).

EMERY, JOHN: King John (**KJ**).

ERICSON, JUNE: A Fairy (**MND**), Mopsa (**WT**).

EVERHART, REX: Cobbler and 1st Citizen (**JC**), Stephano (**T**).

FITZGERALD, GERALDINE: Gertrude (**H**).

FOCH, NINA: Isabella (**MM**), Katherine (**TS**), Isabella (**MM-Ph**), Katherina (**TS-Ph**).

FRID, JOHN: Chatillon (**KJ**), Servant to Angelo (**MM**), Huntsman (**TS**), Cypriot Sergeant (**O**), Salerio (**MOV**), Sexton (**MA**), Sexton (**MA-tour**).

GATES, LARRY: Brabantio (**O**), Duke of Venice (**MOV**), Dogberry (**MA**), Dogberry (**MA-tour**).

GEER, WILL: Antonio (**MA-tour**), 1st Gravedigger and Francisco (**H**), Snout (**MND**), Old Shepherd (**WT**).

GEIRINGER, ROBERT: Lepidus and Legarius (**JC**), Captain (**T**).

GERSTEN, BERNARD: Stage Manager (**O**), (**MOV**), (**MA**), (**MA-tour**), (**H**), (**MND**), (**WT**).

HACHA, ROBERT: Artemidorus and Cicero (**JC**), Alonso (**T**).

HAMILTON, ROGER: Decius Brutus and Young Cato (**JC**), Adrian (**T**).

HARRELSON, HELEN: Blanche (**KJ**).

HARRON, DONALD: Lewis (**KJ**), Claudio (**MM**), Lucentio (**TS**), Bassanio (**MOV**), Verges and Messenger (**MA**).

HARTLEY, MARIETTE: Perdita (replacement) (**WT**).

HATFIELD, HURD: Julius Caesar (**JC**), Gonzalo (**T**).

HAVOC, JUNE: Titania (**MND**).

HEPBURN, KATHARINE: Portia (**MOV**), Beatrice (**MA**), Beatrice (**MA-tour**).

HICKEY, WILLIAM: 2nd Gravedigger (**H**), Flute (**MND**), Young Shepherd (**WT**).

HINES, PATRICK: Lord Bigot (**KJ**), Friar Peter (**MM**), Baptista (**TS**), Friar Peter (**MM-Ph**), Baptista (**TS-Ph**), Friar Francis (**MA-tour**), Rosencrantz (**H**), Egeus (**MND**), Antigonus (**WT**).

HYMAN, EARLE: Soothsayer and Pindarus (**JC**), Boatswain (**T**), Melun (**KJ**), Othello (**O**), Prince of Morocco (**MOV**), Horatio (**H**), Philostrate (**MND**), Autolycus (**WT**).

JANNEY, BEN: Messenger *and* Dardanius (**JC**), Stage Manager (**JC**), (**T**), (**MM**), (**KJ**), (**TS**).

JANNEY, LEON: Elbow (**MM-Ph**).

KANE, WHITFORD: Citizen of Angiers (**KJ**), Abhorson (**MM**), Vincentio *and* 1st Player (**TS**).

KASDAN, MICHAEL: Servant (**MA-tour**), Asst. Stage Manager (**H**), (**MND**), (**WT**), Cornelius *and* A Sailor (**H**), Gaoler *and* Mariner (**WT**).

KELLIN, MIKE: Christopher Sly (**TS**), Christopher Sly (**TS-Ph**).

KENNEDY, MICHAEL: Balthazar (**MOV**).

KINNELL, GERTRUDE: Mistress Overdone (**MM-Ph**).

LEAF, PAUL: Asst. Stage Manager (**KJ**), (**MM**), (**TS**), Stage Manager (**MM-Ph**), (**TS-Ph**).

LENROW, BERNARD: Trebonius *and* Messala (**JC**).

LLOYD, NORMAN: Lucio (**MM**), Lucio (**MM-Ph**).

LLOYD, SUSAN: Page (**TS**).

LORD, BARBARA: Bianca (**TS**), Bianca (**TS-Ph**).

LUPINO, RICHARD: Cypriot Officer (**O**), Lorenzo (**MOV**), 1st Watchman (**MA**).

MARCHAND, NANCY: Paulina (**WT**).

MASSEY, RAYMOND: Marcus Brutus (**JC**), Prospero (**T**).

MATHEWS, WALTER: Marullus (**JC**).

McDOWALL, RODDY: Octavius Caesar (**JC**), Ariel (**T**).

MEISER, EDITH: Queen Elinor (**KJ**), Francisca (**MM**).

MERLIN, JOANNA: Emilia (**WT**).

METCALFE, GERALD: Popilius Lena *and* Clitus (**JC**), Francisco (**T**).

MILTON, DAVID: Borachio (**MA**), Soldier (**MA-tour**).

MORK, DONALD: Lucius (**JC**).

MOSS, ARNOLD: King Philip (**KJ**), The Duke (**MM**), The Duke (**MM-Ph**).

MYERS, JOSEPH: Soldier (**MA-tour**).

NARIZZANO, DINO: Herald (**O**), 1st Soldier (**MA-tour**).

NETTLETON, LOIS: Nerissa (**MOV**), Hero (**MA**).

OBERLIN, RUSSELL: Stephano (**MOV**), Balthazar (**MA**), A Master of Revels (**MND**).

OLSON, JAMES: Titinius (**JC**), Guildenstern (**H**), Demetrius (**MND**), Archidamus (**WT**).

PALANCE, JACK: Cassius (**JC**), Caliban (**T**).

PLUMMER, CHRISTOPHER: Marcus Antonius (**JC**), Ferdinand (**T**).

RABB, ELLIS: Froth (**MM-Ph**), Pedant (**TS-Ph**), Verges (**MA-tour**), Player King (**H**), Starveling (**MND**), Camillo (**WT**).

RAGIN, JOHN: Bernardo, Norwegian Captain *and* Priest (**H**), Cleomenes (**WT**).

ROBERTS, PERNELL: Earl of Pembroke (**KJ**), Barnardine (**MM**), Petruchio (**TS**), Petruchio (**TS-Ph**).

ROLF, FREDERICK: Pedant (**TS**).

ROMER, TOMI: Lady Faulconbridge (**KJ**), Mistress Overdone (**MM**), Hostess (**TS**).

ROWLES, POLLY: Calpurnia (**JC**).

RUSSELL, BYRON: Vincentio *and* 1st Player (**TS-Ph**).

RYAN, NANCY: Asst. Stage Manager (**JC**), (**T**).

SAUNDERS, PAMELA: A Lusty Widow (**TS**), Francisca (**MM-Ph**), Hostess *and* A Lusty Widow (**TS-Ph**).

SHAYNE, ALAN: Flavius, Cinna the Poet *and* Strato (**JC**), Sebastian (**T**).

SHERMAN, HIRAM: Hubert de Burgh (**KJ**), Pompey (**MM**), Pompey (**MM-Ph**), Polonius (**H**), Bottom (**MND**), 3rd Gentleman *and* Shepherd (**WT**).

SHORT, SYLVIA: Mariana (**MM**).

SKLAR, ALAN: Chatillon (**KJ**).

SMITH, KENT: Angelo (**MM**).

STEFFAN, JUDITH: Servant (**MA-tour**).

STILLER, JERRY: Publius, 2nd Citizen *and* A Carpenter (**JC**), Trinculo (**T**) Barnardine (**MM-Ph**), Biondello (**TS-Ph**).

STREETER, RHODEN: Arthur (**KJ**).

SULLIVAN, BRIAN: A Boy (**MM**).

SWENSON, INGA: Ophelia (**H**), Helena (**MND**), Perdita (**WT**).

THOMAS, POWYS: Escalus (**MM-Ph**).

THOMPSON, SADA: Emilia (**O**), Margaret (**MA**), Margaret (**MA-tour**).

TOR, DON: Osric (**H**), Archidamus (**WT**).

TRYTLER, PETER: Servant (**MA-tour**).

WALTZER, JACK: Biondello (**TS**), 3rd Watchman (**MA-tour**).

WARING, RICHARD: Angelo (**MM-Ph**), Cassio (**O**), Antonio (**MOV**), Don John (**MA**), Don John (**MA-tour**), Fortinbras (**H**), Oberon (**MND**), Polixenes (**WT**).

WEAVER, FRITZ: Casca (**JC**), Antonio (**T**), Philip Faulconbridge (**KJ**), Gremio (**TS**), Hamlet (**H**).

WHITNEY, DOROTHY: Iris (**T**).

WICKWIRE, NANCY: Mariana (**MM-Ph**), Hippolyta (**MND**), Hermione (**WT**).

WOODMAN, WILLIAM: Servant (**MA-tour**), Asst. Stage Manager (**MA-tour**), (**H**), (**MND**), (**WT**).

ZEISLER, PETER: Stage Manager (**JC**), (**T**), (**KJ**), (**MM**), (**TS**).

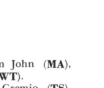

THE Festival company's roster, for its first four years, numbers over one hundred. Individual biographical data of such a large segment of Actors' Equity Association cannot be given here. Yet it is precisely these individual histories of professional accomplishment and the variety of background and artistic achievement they represent which constitute ASFTA's greatest strength. All these actors, seasoned professionals as well as neophytes, have contributed to the total achievement of the Festival. All of them have brought to this work not only their special talents but their diverse experience: music hall and "method," night-club entertainment and contemporary drama, movies, TV and *avant-garde* theatre. This staggering diversity, so characteristic of the American stage, has been turned from a liability to an asset by the richness and power of Shakespeare's plays and the challenge of the roles which members of the Festival company have had the opportunity of playing in them.

Of the Festival's players some have been celebrated stars, some promoted apprentices. Katharine Hepburn brought with her a glamour unique in American show business: for twenty-five years an international film and stage star, she had recently toured Australia with the Old Vic. Alfred Drake, who came to Stratford to play Iago and Benedick, was best known to the public for his Broadway triumphs in *Oklahoma!, Kismet* and a somewhat modified Shakespearean item called *Kiss Me, Kate*. Mariette Hartley, Dino Narrizano and Barbara Lord were inducted into the professional company directly from their classes in the Academy.

June Havoc, Raymond Massey, Geraldine Fitzgerald, John Emery, Mildred Dunnock, Nina Foch, Kent Smith— vaudeville, the "legitimate" theater, television, motion pictures here and abroad— all these had prepared them for their Festival appearances. William Hickey arrived direct from a musical comedy, June Ericson from singing in a basement *boite*. The collegiate drama festivals have provided a rich ground of experience: Ellis Rabb, a veteran of Antioch's Shakespeare seasons, came to Stratford with the rare distinction of having appeared, in one role or another, in every Shakespeare play. John Frid was a member of the company *before* he had completed his work at Yale, and during the 1958 season the Carnegie Tech drama alumni working in Stratford numbered six. Between college and company there were years of experience on and off Broadway, in summer stock, television, films— all the media that allow expression for the actor in America. Several have shared the experience of the Old Vic Theatre School, the Royal Academy of Dramatic Art or the Actors Studio.

The "invasion" from Canada had a vital influence on the company. Donald Harron, an original member of the Ontario festival, joined ASFTA for the 1956 and 1957 seasons. Christopher Plummer reversed the procedure and moved from the 1955 season in Connecticut to his native Canada and eminence with the festival there. Richard Easton started his Stratford careers in Ontario, went to England to perform at the Memorial Theatre and joined ASFTA in 1957, completing the circuit. John Colicos, also of Montreal, made his first major Shakespearean appearance with the Old Vic, followed that with some Hollywood Westerns before playing Gratiano, the first of a series of roles which culminated in Leontes, in *The Winter's Tale*.

Other characteristic ASFTA players are:

JACQUELINE BROOKES, who joined the Festival in 1956. She had studied in London at the Royal Academy of Dramatic Art on a Fulbright scholarship. Off Broadway she won praise and awards in *The Cretan Woman, The White Devil* and *The Clandestine Marriage;* on Broadway, she appeared in *Tiger at the Gates;* in Paris, with Judith Anderson in *Medea.* Her first roles with ASFTA were Blanche in *King John* and Juliet in *Measure for Measure.* During the New York Phoenix Theatre season, she played the title role in *The Duchess of Malfi.* In the 1957 season, she moved to the major role of Desdemona in *Othello;* in *Much Ado about Nothing,* at Stratford and on tour, she played Ursula.

JACQUELINE BROOKES
[*Above*] as Ursula (*Much Ado— 1957*); [*Below from left to right*] as Juliet (*Measure — 1956*), as the Duchess (*Duchess of Malfi — 1957*), as Desdemona (*Othello — 1957*), and as Blanche (*King John — 1956*)

MORRIS CARNOVSKY: [*Counter-clockwise*] as Salisbury (*King John — 1956*), as Peter Quince (*Midsummer — 1958*), as Shylock (*Merchant — 1957*), as Claudius (*Hamlet — 1958*), as Grumio (*Shrew — 1956*), as Antonio (*Much Ado — 1957*), and as the Provost (*Measure — 1956*)

MORRIS CARNOVSKY— an actor with years of achievement in the American theatre— played his first Shakespearean role when he joined the Festival in 1956. He appeared as Salisbury in *King John*, the next night as the Provost in *Measure for Measure*, and later in the season romped as a tattered Grumio in *The Taming of the Shrew*. Preceding this were years as a mainstay of many Theatre Guild and Group Theatre productions— *Saint Joan*, *Marco's Millions*, *Men in White*, *Awake and Sing* and other Broadway appearances ranging from Rostand to Coward. Mr. Carnovsky's virtuosity is almost legend, and his background as a teacher of acting includes New York and Hollywood, where at the Actors' Lab he also directed. In 1957, Mr. Carnovsky distinguished both himself and the Festival with his performance of Shylock. His reception in that role is one of ASFTA's proudest success stories. That same season he created a bouncing, babbling Uncle Antonio in *Much Ado* and made the minute role one of the play's highlights. In 1958, he carried the

practice of versatility in repertory further with his portrayal of Claudius in *Hamlet* and a sweet-and-sour Peter Quince in *A Midsummer Night's Dream.* Of equal importance to the Festival are the classes in acting which he conducts for the Academy.

PATRICK HINES joined ASFTA after two years with Army Special Services. He appeared in all three plays in the 1956 repertory; the roles became progressively larger as the season took shape. He repeated his performance as the Friar in *Measure for Measure* and Baptista in *The Taming of the Shrew* during the Phoenix Theatre engagement. In 1957 the lure of half a dozen juicy roles with the Toledo Shakespeare Festival could not be matched at Stratford. He rejoined ASFTA for the tour of *Much Ado about Nothing* and for major roles in the 1958 season. Like other Texan members of the company— including, most recently, Barbara Barrie— Mr. Hines studied with B. Iden Payne.

EARLE HYMAN did not tour with *Much Ado about Nothing.* This is noteworthy because it is the only ASFTA engagement to date in which he has not participated. Mr. Hyman was the first actor to walk onto the Festival stage, and he has appeared there every season since. From the Soothsayer in *Julius Caesar* he moved through many parts to the title role in *Othello.* In 1958 he was Horatio in *Hamlet,* Autolycus in *The Winter's Tale* and Philostrate in *Dream,* thus demonstrating the range and variety of repertory's demands and opportunities. Before and between ASFTA engagements there has been much activity for him— long runs in New York and London in *Anna Lucasta;* major Shakespearean roles at the New York City Center, Howard University, Antioch, the Shakespearewrights; on Broadway, *No Time for Sergeants* and the title role in *Mister Johnson.* Mr. Hyman typifies the young American actor whose talents the Festival Theatre is privileged to develop.

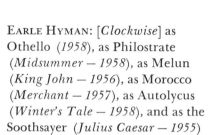

EARLE HYMAN: [*Clockwise*] as Othello (*1958*), as Philostrate (*Midsummer — 1958*), as Melun (*King John — 1956*), as Morocco (*Merchant — 1957*), as Autolycus (*Winter's Tale — 1958*), and as the Soothsayer (*Julius Caesar — 1955*)

INGA SWENSON: [*Left to right*] as Ophelia (*Hamlet — 1958*), as Perdita (*Winter's Tale —1958*), as Helena (*Midsummer — 1958*)

INGA SWENSON— a more recent acquisition. In four years she has made the hop from Shakespeare in a church basement, where she made her New York theatre debut as Olivia in the Shakespearewrights' *Twelfth Night,* to leading roles at the American Shakespeare Festival. There were some stops en route— at the Versailles as a night-club singer, on Broadway as one of the *New Faces of 1956* and later as Princess Charlotte in *The First Gentleman.* She played three major roles in the 1958 season— Helena in *Dream,* Perdita in *The Winter's Tale* and Ophelia.

FRITZ WEAVER came to the Festival via the University of Chicago and studies in physics, the Barter Theatre (where he met and married Sylvia Short, also an ASFTA company member), Group 20 and several Off-Broadway roles, including Flamineo in *The White Devil,* for which he won the Clarence Derwent Award. Denis Carey, the Festival's director in 1955, saw this production and Mr. Weaver was one of the first actors to be engaged. He appeared in both plays of the initial season. During the following winter he was seen on Broadway in *The Chalk Garden* and returned to Stratford in 1956 to play the cynical soldier of fortune, Faulconbridge, and a wonderfully decrepit, avaricious Gremio. In 1958 Mr. Weaver resumed his position in the Festival company, this time to play only one role— Hamlet.

THERE ARE many other such histories: Richard Waring's association with Eva Le Gallienne and the American Repertory

Theatre; Norman Lloyd's startling success with the Federal and Mercury theatres; Will Geer's early years with the Stewart–Walker Company and his career as juvenile lead with Mrs. Fiske; Arnold Moss's beginnings as a speech teacher at Brooklyn College before achieving Broadway success; the concert career of Russell Oberlin, the country's most celebrated counter-tenor; Hiram Sherman, another Mercury graduate whose adroitness has led successive critics to speculate that "Shakespeare must have had him in mind when he wrote" first Pompey, then bully Bottom; Nancy Wickwire's combination of Old Vic training and TV soap-opera experience; Jack Bittner's early laboratory experiments as a pre-med student, which led him to a theatrical career; Roddy McDowall's beginnings as a child star in movies; Larry Gates's former employment with the Live Stock Commission of South St. Paul, Minnesota, which may have influenced his creation of the Western Dogberry.

No record of the company would be complete that did not mention the final engagements of two actors whose association with the American Shakespeare Festival has added stature and honor to the organization. Whitford Kane, in his seventy-fifth year, joined the new Festival company "because it needed a little life!" He provided considerable excitement and delight during the summer of 1956. Appearing in all three plays, he mounted to the second story of the walls of Angiers each night of *King John* and negotiated the "ramps" and "rakes" better than most of his juniors. There was not one missed performance during the summer in spite of recurrent attacks of the illness which was to end his life three months later. Stanley Bell was a member of a British acting family and represented the eighteenth generation of a line which traced its ancestry to members of Shakespeare's Globe Theatre company. He joined the Festival in 1956 and performed in a variety of roles that year and the next. His worldly Escalus, the austere Doge in *Othello*, the rattling Aragon in *The Merchant of Venice* and the elegant Don Pedro in *Much Ado about Nothing* are vivid recollections.

These and many more are the actors and actresses who have helped to build the American Shakespeare Festival company. Free to leave for other engagements and welcomed back when the repertory invites their return, they form a diversified but integrated community of actors devoted to the performance of the world's greatest plays, in a theatre they have rightly come to regard as their own.

The Master of the Revels:
RUSSELL OBERLIN

·IV·
The Academy

The Theatre, the Company, the Academy— all three are parts
of the same vision. As necessary to the growth and existence of
the Festival as its physical home and its actors are its sources of
new talent. A school provides the means for developing that talent, and though the Academy of the American Shakespeare Festival has been altered considerably in structure and approach
during its brief history, it has consistently tried to prepare American actors for work in a classical repertory.

John Burrell was named Director of the Academy in 1954,
and one of his first activities was to organize a professional training course in New York. Over five hundred actors applied. The
free training in Shakespeare and the bright prospect of a Festival
84 acting company to be recruited from among the members of the

professional program were considerable attractions. Forty actors were chosen, and the groups they formed worked through the spring. During the 1955 summer season, the Academy supervised an apprentice acting group at Stratford and presented a "student" production of *Much Ado about Nothing* with a cast augmented by young actors from outside the Festival.

The training course for professionals was resumed in New York after the close of the season and continued through the winter. Arnold Moss, a veteran of many native Shakespearean productions, joined Mr. Burrell in conducting the Academy's activities.

Classes were held in New York, first in rented rehearsal halls and later in more permanent and spacious premises. Under the personal supervision and guidance of the Academy's Executive Director, Helen Menken— from the first a most energetic and imaginative champion of the Academy— a warehouse was transformed into a theatre school, complete with stage and auditorium.

However, an exclusively professional workshop seemed an inadequate complement to a company which was now being organized as the essential element of the Festival's operation. It was becoming clear that a more basic approach to the training program was needed. During the summer of 1956, some twenty students were enrolled in a second apprentice program supervised by Robert Butman of Haverford College. But it was not until the next winter that the Academy assumed its full responsibility to the Festival.

In consultation with the trustees, John Houseman appointed his associate, Jack Landau, a former staff-member of the Old Vic Theatre School in London, to study the Academy's problems and formulate a program of training more closely related to the future needs of the organization. In February 1957 an experimental term was inaugurated. The enrollment was limited to fifteen students, carefully selected with respect to previous training and experience and with a view to their potential development. The staff of instructors included Morris Carnovsky and Mitchell Agruss of the Festival company, Fanny Bradshaw (Speech), Rod Colbin (Fencing) and John Butler (Dance).

On the terrace, apprentice actors

In the Festival Theatre, Teachers and Directors Program, lecture series

MICHEL SAINT-DENIS [*Second from left*]

SIR JOHN GIELGUD

JEAN VILAR with ROSAMOND GILDER

Shakespeare provided the text and determined the curriculum throughout. This presupposed a consideration of acting and interpretation that is characterized by virtuosity as well as style; by a controlled body, voice and imagination; by an awareness of period, ways of life and cultural background.

Since that experimental term, the Academy has been able to expand its work and offer its instruction to increasing numbers of acting students. At the same time it has become possible to reinstate classes for professionals and to relate them to the Academy's program. Here established actors may have the opportunity of developing and expanding their already acknowledged talents through work in the classics.

To augment the work in classrooms, the Academy conducts a series of public lectures on subjects related to its work. Michel St. Denis, the eminent European director and founder of the Old Vic Theatre School; Sir John Gielgud; Jean Vilar, director of France's Théâtre National Populaire; John Houseman and Lincoln Kirstein are some of the speakers who have addressed Academy audiences. These lectures have become a part of the professional theatre scene in New York.

During the summer season at Stratford, the acting apprentices enrolled in the Academy have the opportunity of working with the members of the acting company in one or more of the productions. The range of parts they are permitted to fill varies with their talents, and each season a small number of them are promoted to full company status. When the national tour of *Much Ado about Nothing* was organized, no less than nine of the previous summer's apprentices were signed as actors and formally made the move from Academy to Company.

In the summer of 1958, the first Teachers' and Directors' Program, designed for high-school, college and community craftsmen, was conducted in association with the Yale Shakespeare Institute and the University of Bridgeport's College of Education.

In addition to lectures and seminars on Elizabethan background and the producing and teaching of Shakespeare, the program included attendance at rehearsals and performances at the Festival theatre. In this program, the Academy hopes to reinforce its preparation of a generation of American classical actors by fostering a livelier appreciation of Shakespeare in schools and communities across the country.

·V·
The Record

PROGRAMS

1955 — STRATFORD, CONNECTICUT

Premiere July 12th

JULIUS CAESAR

by William Shakespeare

Directed by DENIS CAREY
Scenery Designed by HORACE ARMISTEAD
Costumes by ROBERT FLETCHER
Lighting by JEAN ROSENTHAL
Music by LEHMAN ENGEL

CAST OF CHARACTERS
(in order of appearance)

Julius Caesar . . . . HURD HATFIELD

Octavius Caesar ⎱ Triumvirs after . . RODDY McDOWALL
Marcus Antonius ⎰ the Death of / Julius Caesar — CHRISTOPHER PLUMMER

Cicero ⎱ . . . . ROBERT HACHA
Publius / Senators . . . . . . JERRY STILLER
Popilius Lena ⎰ . . . . GERALD METCALFE
Marcus Brutus . . . . RAYMOND MASSEY
Cassius . . . . . JACK PALANCE
Casca ⎱ Conspir- . . . . FRITZ WEAVER
Trebonius / ators . . . . BERN LENROW
Ligarius ⎰ against . . GROBERT GEIRINGER
Decius Brutus / Julius . . . . ROGER HAMILTON
Metellus Cimber / Caesar . . . . . PETER DONAT
Cinna . . . . . JACK CANNON
Flavius ⎱ . . . . ALAN SHAYNE
Marullus / Tribunes . . . . WALTER MATHEWS
A Cobbler . . . . REX EVERHART
A Carpenter . . . . JERRY STILLER
Lucius, servant to Brutus . . . . DONALD MORK
Artemidorus, a teacher of rhetoric . . . . ROBERT HACHA
A Soothsayer . . . . EARLE HYMAN
A Messenger from Antony . . . . BEN JANNEY

Cinna, a poet . . . . ALAN SHAYNE
Lucilius ⎱ . . . . PETER DONAT
Titinius / Officers and . . . JAMES OLSON
Messala / Friends to . . . BERN LENROW
Young Cato / Brutus and . . . ROGER HAMILTON
Volumnius ⎰ Cassius . . . . JACK CANNON
Clitus ⎱ Soldiers in . . . GERALD METCALFE
Strato / Brutus' . . . . . ALAN SHAYNE
Dardanius ⎰ Army . . . . . BEN JANNEY
Pindarus, servant to Cassius . . . . . . EARLE HYMAN
Calpurnia, wife to Caesar . . . . . . POLLY ROWLES
Portia, wife to Brutus . . . . . . LEORA DANA
Servant to Caesar . . . . WALTER MATHEWS
Servant to Octavius Caesar . . . . . GERALD METCALFE
First Citizen . . . . REX EVERHART
Second Citizen . . . . JERRY STILLER
Third Citizen . . . . JACK CANNON
Fourth Citizen . . . . ROBERT HACHA
Fifth Citizen . . . . DOROTHY WHITNEY
Sixth Citizen . . . . BEN JANNEY
Messenger . . . . WALTER MATHEWS

Scene: Rome and Philippi

THERE WILL BE TWO TEN-MINUTE INTERMISSIONS

Conductor for Julius Caesar *is Frederick Smithson*

Nymphs, Reapers, Shades, Mariners:

Art Alisi, Benjamin Andrews, Jacqui Blauner, Eleanor Jean Brown, Jonathan Bush, Louis D'Almeida, Tommy Daniels, Iver Fischman, Edmund Kean, Harold Kirschner, Paul Kennedy, Susan Ketcham, Simm Landres, Michael Learned, Rebecca Lombard, Helen McGrail, Mary Perine, Helen Roach, Edward Simonian, Henry Southwick, Polly Welch, Joseph Zeigler.

STUDENT-APPRENTICES OF SHAKESPEARE ACADEMY COURSES APPEARING IN *JULIUS CAESAR:*

Michael Ahern, Art Alisi, Benjamin Andrews, Jacqui Blauner, Eleanor Jean Brown, Jonathan Bush, Pola Chasman, Nathaniel Cooper, Louis D'Almeida, Tommy Daniels, Iver Fischman, Ann Gerard, Edmund Kean, Paul Kennedy, Susan Ketcham, Harold Kirschner, Simm Landres, Michael Learned, Rebecca Lombard, Helen McGrail, Mary Perine, Helen Roach, Edward Simonian, Henry Southwick, Polly Welsh, Al White, Jr., Dorothy Whitney, Joseph Zeigler.

1955 — STRATFORD, CONNECTICUT

Premiere August 1

THE TEMPEST

by William Shakespeare

Directed by DENIS CAREY
Scenery Designed by HORACE ARMISTEAD
Costumes by ROBERT FLETCHER
Lighting by JEAN ROSENTHAL
Ballet Masque by GEORGE BALANCHINE
Music by ERNST BACON

CAST OF CHARACTERS
(in order of appearance)

Alonso, King of Naples	ROBERT HACHA
Sebastian, his brother	ALAN SHAYNE
Prospero, the right Duke of Milan	RAYMOND MASSEY
Antonio, his brother,	
the usurping Duke of Milan	FRITZ WEAVER
Ferdinand, son to the King of Naples	CHRISTOPHER PLUMMER
Gonzalo, an honest old councillor	HURD HATFIELD
Adrian ⎱ Lords	ROGER HAMILTON
Francisco ⎰	GERALD METCALFE
Caliban, a savage and deformed slave	JACK PALANCE
Trinculo, a jester	JERRY STILLER
Stephano, a drunken butler	REX EVERHART
Ship-Master	ROBERT GEIRINGER
Boatswain	EARLE HYMAN
Miranda, daughter to Prospero	JOAN CHANDLER
Ariel, an airy spirit	RODDY McDOWALL
Iris ⎱	DOROTHY WHITNEY
Ceres ⎰ Spirits	LEORA DANA
Juno ⎰	VIRGINIA BAKER

Scene: An uninhabited island

THERE WILL BE ONE INTERMISSION OF FIFTEEN MINUTES

Conductor for The Tempest *is Andrew Heath*

1956 — STRATFORD, CONNECTICUT

Premiere June 26th

KING JOHN

by William Shakespeare

Directed by JOHN HOUSEMAN *and* JACK LANDAU
Scenery and Costumes by ROUBEN TER-ARUTUNIAN
Lighting by JEAN ROSENTHAL
Music by VIRGIL THOMSON

CAST OF CHARACTERS
(in order of appearance)

King John	JOHN EMERY
Chatillon, Ambassador from France	JOHN FRID
Queen Elinor, mother of King John	EDITH MEISER
Earl of Salisbury	MORRIS CARNOVSKY
Hubert de Burgh,	
chamberlain to King John	HIRAM SHERMAN
Earl of Pembroke	PERNELL ROBERTS
Lord Bigot	PATRICK HINES
Robert Faulconbridge	WILLIAM COTTRELL
Philip Faulconbridge, his bastard brother	FRITZ WEAVER
Lady Faulconbridge, their mother	TOMI ROMER
Lewis, the French Dauphin	DONALD HARRON
King Philip of France	ARNOLD MOSS
Arthur, Duke of Brittany	RHODEN STREETER
Archduke of Austria	RICHARD DURHAM
Constance, mother of Arthur	MILDRED DUNNOCK
Citizen of Angiers	WHITFORD KANE
Melun, a lord	EARLE HYMAN
Blanche of Spain	JACQUELINE BROOKES
Cardinal Pandulph	KENDALL CLARK
Messenger	STEPHEN RANDALL
Prince Henry, son of King John	MITCHELL AGRUSS
Executioner	ROD COLBIN

Soldiers, Citizens, and Monks: Peter Bogdanovitch, Clarence Burbage, Sebastian Brook, Gary Glass, Harvey Grossman, Robert Heide, Richard Kenyon, Simm Landris, Michael Lindsay-Hogg, Charles Meier, Michael Miller, David Milton, James Moran, Robert Morris, Joseph Myers, Ted Otis, David Pierce, Stephen Randall, Carlos Salgado, Alan Sklar, James Tuttle, Jack Waltzer, Joseph Zeigler.

(Battle Scenes staged by Rod Colbin)

The play is laid in England and France

THERE WILL BE ONE INTERMISSION

1956 — STRATFORD, CONNECTICUT

Premiere June 27th

MEASURE FOR MEASURE

by William Shakespeare

Directed by JOHN HOUSEMAN *and* JACK LANDAU
Scenery and Costumes by ROUBEN TER-ARUTUNIAN
Lighting by JEAN ROSENTHAL
Music by VIRGIL THOMSON

CAST OF CHARACTERS
(in order of appearance)

The Duke of Vienna	ARNOLD MOSS
Escalus, a lord	STANLEY BELL
Angelo, the deputy	KENT SMITH
Friar Peter	PATRICK HINES
Mistress Overdone, a bawd	TOMI ROMER
Pompey, her tapster	HIRAM SHERMAN
Lucio	NORMAN LLOYD
First Gentleman	MITCHELL AGRUSS
Second Gentleman	ROD COLBIN
Provost	MORRIS CARNOVSKY
Claudio	DONALD HARRON
Juliet, affianced to Claudio	JACQUELINE BROOKES
Isabella, sister of Claudio	NINA FOCH
Francisca, a nun	EDITH MEISER
Justice	RICHARD DURHAM
Elbow, a constable	WILLIAM COTTRELL
Froth	HARVEY GROSSMAN
Woman of the streets	PAMELA SAUNDERS
Servant to Angelo	JOHN FRID
Mariana	SYLVIA SHORT
Abhorson, an executioner	WHITFORD KANE
Barnardine	PERNELL ROBERTS
A Boy	DAVID COLSON

Ministers, Chamberlains and Townspeople: Members of The American Shakespeare Festival Academy.

The play is laid in Vienna

THERE WILL BE TWO INTERMISSIONS

1956 — STRATFORD, CONNECTICUT

Premiere August 5th

THE TAMING OF THE SHREW

by William Shakespeare

Directed by NORMAN LLOYD
Basic Setting by ROUBEN TER-ARUTUNIAN
Costumes and Color by DOROTHY JEAKINS
Lighting by JEAN ROSENTHAL
Music by IRWIN BAZELON

CAST OF CHARACTERS

THE INDUCTION:

Christopher Sly, a tinker	MIKE KELLIN
Hostess	TOMI ROMER
A Lord	STANLEY BELL
Page	SUSAN LLOYD
First Player	WHITFORD KANE
Huntsman & Servant to the Lord	JOHN FRID
Huntsman & Servant to the Lord	CHARLES MEIER
Huntsman & Servant to the Lord	JAMES TUTTLE

THE PLAYERS:

Lucentio, son to Vincentio	DONALD HARRON
Tranio, servant to Lucentio	MITCHELL AGRUSS
Biondello, servant to Lucentio	JACK WALTZER
Baptista, a rich gentleman of Padua	PATRICK HINES
Katherina, the Shrew, daughter to Baptista	NINA FOCH
Bianca, also daughter to Baptista	BARBARA LORD
Gremio, suitor to Bianca	FRITZ WEAVER
Hortensio, suitor to Bianca	KENDALL CLARK
Grumio, servant to Petruchio	MORRIS CARNOVSKY
Petruchio	PERNELL ROBERTS
Servant to Baptista	MICHAEL MILLER
Servant to Baptista	CLARENCE BURBAGE
Adam	ROD COLBIN
Curtis, servant to Petruchio	HARVEY GROSSMAN
Nathaniel, servant to Petruchio	JAMES MORAN
Peter, servant to Petruchio	MICHAEL LINDSAY-HOGG
Joseph, servant to Petruchio	JOSEPH ZIEGLER
Nicholas, servant to Petruchio	DAVID MILTON
Sugarsop, servant to Petruchio	ROBERT MORRIS
Tailor	WILLIAM COTTRELL
Haberdasher	SIMM LANDRES
Pedant, impersonating Vincentio	FREDERICK ROLF
Vincentio	WHITFORD KANE
A Lusty Widow	PAMELA SAUNDERS

*The scene is Padua
and in Petruchio's house in the country*

THERE WILL BE TWO INTERMISSIONS

Musical Director (1956) Francois Jaroschy

1957 — PHOENIX THEATRE — NEW YORK

January 22 — February 17

MEASURE FOR MEASURE

by William Shakespeare

Directed by JOHN HOUSEMAN *and* JACK LANDAU
Scenery and Costumes by ROUBEN TER-ARUTUNIAN
Production and Lighting by JEAN ROSENTHAL
Music by VIRGIL THOMSON

CAST OF CHARACTERS
(in order of appearance)

The Duke of Vienna	ARNOLD MOSS
Escalus, a lord	POWYS THOMAS
Angelo, the deputy	RICHARD WARING

Friar Peter	. . . .	PATRICK HINES
Mistress Overdone, a bawd	. . . . .	GERTRUDE KINNELL
Pomey, her tapster	. . . .	HIRAM SHERMAN
Lucio	. . . .	NORMAN LLOYD
First Gentleman	. . . .	MITCHELL AGRUSS
Second Gentleman	. . . . . .	TUCKER ASHWORTH
Provost	. . . .	MORRIS CARNOVSKY
Claudio	. . . .	RICHARD EASTON
Juliet, affianced to Claudio	. . . .	JACQUELINE BROOKES
Isabella, sister to Claudio	. . . . . .	NINA FOCH
Francisca, a nun	. . . .	PAMELA SAUNDERS
Elbow, a constable	. . . .	LEON JANNEY
Froth	. . . .	ELLIS RABB
Servant to Angelo	. . . .	TUCKER ASHWORTH
Mariana	. . . .	NANCY WICKWIRE
A Boy	. . . .	BRIAN SULLIVAN
Abhorson, an executioner	. . . . .	WILLIAM COTTRELL
Barnardine	. . . .	JERRY STILLER

Ministers, Chamberlains and Citizens: James Cahill, Gary Glass, John Ragin, Michael Miller, Robert Morris, Joseph Meyers, Charles Meier, Pat McAteer, Jill Livsey, Vivian Paszamont, Anita Michals, Marion Casprey, Pamela Saunders, Edwin Sherin, Barbara Lord, David Pierce, Anthony Holland, David Milton, James Ray.

The play is laid in Vienna

THERE WILL BE TWO INTERMISSIONS

1957 — PHOENIX THEATRE — NEW YORK

February 20 — March 10

THE TAMING OF THE SHREW

by William Shakespeare

Directed by NORMAN LLOYD
Festival Stage by ROUBEN TER-ARUTUNIAN
Costumes by DOROTHY JEAKINS
Lighting and Additional Decor by JEAN ROSENTHAL
Music by IRWIN BAZELON

CAST OF CHARACTERS
(in order of appearance)

THE INDUCTION:

Christopher Sly, a tinker	. . . . . .	MIKE KELLIN
Hostess	. . . .	PAMELA SAUNDERS
A Lord	. . . .	LOUIS EDMONDS
Bartholomew, a page	. . . . . .	SUSAN LLOYD
First Player	. . . .	BYRON RUSSELL
Huntsman and Servant to the Lord	.	TUCKER ASHWORTH
Huntsman and Servant to the Lord	. .	WILLIAM COTTRELL

THE PLAYERS:

Lucentio, son to Vincentio	. . . . .	RICHARD EASTON
Tranio, servant to Lucentio	. . . .	MITCHELL AGRUSS
Biondello, servant to Lucentio	. . . .	JERRY STILLER
Baptista, a rich gentleman of Padua	. . .	PATRICK HINES
Katherina, the Shrew, daughter to Baptista	. .	NINA FOCH
Bianca, also daughter to Baptista	. . . .	BARBARA LORD

Gremio, suitor to Bianca	. . . . . .	PHILIP BOURNEUF
Hortensio, suitor to Bianca	. . . . .	KENDALL CLARK
Grumio, servant to Petruchio	. . . .	MORRIS CARNOVSKY
Petruchio	. . . .	PERNELL ROBERTS
Curtis, servant to Petruchio	. . . .	ROD COLBIN
Nathaniel, servant to Petruchio	. . . .	JAMES CAHILL
Peter, servant to Petruchio	. . .	MICHAEL LINDSAY-HOGG
Joseph, servant to Petruchio	. . . . .	JOSEPH MYERS
Nicholas, servant to Petruchio	. . . . .	DAVID MILTON
Sugarsop, servant to Petruchio	. . . .	ROBERT MORRIS
Tailor	. . . .	WILLIAM COTTRELL
Haberdasher	. . . .	TUCKER ASHWORTH
Pedant, impersonating Vincentio	. . . . .	ELLIS RABB
Vincentio	. . . .	BYRON RUSSELL
A Lusty Widow	. . . .	PAMELA SAUNDERS
Servants to Baptista	. . .	MICHAEL MILLER, CHARLES MEIER

*The scene is Padua
and in Petruchio's house in the country*

THERE WILL BE TWO INTERMISSIONS

1957 — STRATFORD, CONNECTICUT

Premiere June 22nd

OTHELLO

by William Shakespeare

Directed by JOHN HOUSEMAN
Scenery and Costumes by ROUBEN TER-ARUTUNIAN
Lighting by JEAN ROSENTHAL
Music by VIRGIL THOMSON

CAST OF CHARACTERS
(in order of speaking)

Roderigo	. . . .	RICHARD EASTON
Iago	. . . .	ALFRED DRAKE
Brabantio	. . . .	LARRY GATES
Othello	. . . .	EARLE HYMAN
Cassio	. . . .	RICHARD WARING
Gratiano	. . . .	KENDALL CLARK
Duke of Venice	. . . .	STANLEY BELL
1st Senator	. . . .	WILLIAM COTTRELL
Lodovico	. . . .	JOHN COLICOS
Desdemona	. . . .	JACQUELINE BROOKES
Montano	. . . .	JACK BITTNER
Cypriot sergeant	. . . .	JOHN FRID
Cypriot officer	. . . .	RICHARD LUPINO
Cypriot servant	. . . .	MITCHELL AGRUSS
Emilia	. . . .	SADA THOMPSON
Herald	. . . .	DINO NARIZZANO
Bianca	. . . .	OLIVE DEERING

Soldiers, Senators, Servants, Cypriots:
Conrad Bromberg, James Cahill, Harley Clements, Tamara Daniel, Michele La Bombarda, Simm Landres, Michael Lindsay-Hogg, Michael Kasdan, Michael Kennedy, William Long, Jr., Michael Miller, David Milton, Joseph Myers, Ira Rubin, D. J. Sullivan, Jack Waltzer, Gail Warner.

The action of the play takes place in Venice and Cyprus.

THERE WILL BE ONE INTERMISSION

1957 — STRATFORD, CONNECTICUT

Premiere July 10th

THE MERCHANT OF VENICE

by William Shakespeare

Directed by JACK LANDAU
Scenery by ROUBEN TER-ARUTUNIAN
Lighting by JEAN ROSENTHAL
Costumes by MOTLEY
Music by VIRGIL THOMSON

CAST OF CHARACTERS
(in order of speaking)

Antonio	RICHARD WARING
Salerio	JOHN FRID
Salanio	KENDALL CLARK
Bassanio	DONALD HARRON
Lorenzo	RICHARD LUPINO
Gratiano	JOHN COLICOS
Portia	KATHARINE HEPBURN
Nerissa	LOIS NETTLETON
Balthazar	MICHAEL KENNEDY
Shylock	MORRIS CARNOVSKY
Prince of Morocco	EARLE HYMAN
Lancelot Gobbo	RICHARD EASTON
Old Gobbo	WILLIAM COTTRELL
Jessica	DINA DORONNE
Prince of Arragon	STANLEY BELL
Tubal	JACK BITTNER
Stephano	RUSSELL OBERLIN
Duke of Venice	LARRY GATES

Various Attendants, Citizens, Dignitaries:
Conrad Bromberg, James Cahill, Richard Cavett, Harley Clements, Tamara Daniel, Benita Deutsch, Diana Frothingham, Michael Kasdan, Simm Landres, Michele La Bombarda, Michael Lindsay-Hogg, Pamela Linkroum, Susan Lloyd, William Long, Jr., Michael Miller, David Milton, Joe Myers, Dino Narizzano, Vivian Paszamont, Ira Rubin, D. J. Sullivan, Judith Steffan, Peter Trytler, Jack Waltzer, Gail Warner.

The action of the play takes place in Venice and Belmont.

THERE WILL BE TWO INTERMISSIONS

1957 — STRATFORD, CONNECTICUT

Premiere August 7th

MUCH ADO ABOUT NOTHING

by William Shakespeare

Directed by JOHN HOUSEMAN *and* JACK LANDAU
Scenery and Costumes by ROUBEN TER-ARUTUNIAN
Production Supervised by JEAN ROSENTHAL
Lighting by THARON MUSSER
Dances Arranged by JOHN BUTLER
Music by VIRGIL THOMSON

CAST OF CHARACTERS
(in order of speaking)

Leonato	JOHN COLICOS
Messenger	DONALD HARRON
Beatrice	KATHARINE HEPBURN
Hero	LOIS NETTLETON
Don Pedro	STANLEY BELL
Benedick	ALFRED DRAKE
Claudio	RICHARD EASTON
Don John	RICHARD WARING
Conrade	MITCHELL AGRUSS
Borachio	JACK BITTNER
Antonio	MORRIS CARNOVSKY
Balthazar	RUSSELL OBERLIN
Margaret	SADA THOMPSON
Ursula	JACQUELINE BROOKES
Dogberry	LARRY GATES
Verges	DONALD HARRON
First Watchman	RICHARD LUPINO
Second Watchman	WILLIAM COTTRELL
Friar Francis	KENDALL CLARK
Sexton	JOHN FRID

Various Soldiers and Servants:
Conrad Bromberg, James Cahill, Harley Clements, Benita Deutsch, Michael Kasdan, Michele La Bombarda, Michael Lindsay-Hogg, Susan Lloyd, Michael Miller, David Milton, Joe Myers, Dino Narizzano, Ira Rubin, Judith Steffan, D. J. Sullivan, Peter Trytler, Jack Waltzer, Ellen Weston.

The action of the play takes place in and around the Great House of Leonato near Messina.

THERE WILL BE TWO INTERMISSIONS
Musical Director (1957) Francois Jaroschy

ON TOUR: DECEMBER 30, 1957 — MARCH 1, 1958

MUCH ADO ABOUT NOTHING

by William Shakespeare

Directed by JOHN HOUSEMAN *and* JACK LANDAU
Music by VIRGIL THOMSON
Scenery and Costumes by ROUBEN TER-ARUTUNIAN
Lighting by THARON MUSSER
Dances Arranged by JOHN BUTLER

CAST OF CHARACTERS
(in order of speaking)

Leonato	JOHN COLICOS
	(Followed by PATRICK HINES*)*
First Soldier	DINO NARIZZANO
Beatrice	KATHARINE HEPBURN
Hero	DINA DORONNE
Don Pedro	STANLEY BELL
	(Followed by ELLIS RABB*)*
Benedick	ALFRED DRAKE
	(Followed by JOHN COLICOS*)*
Claudio	RICHARD EASTON
Don John	RICHARD WARING
Conrade	MITCHELL AGRUSS
Borachio	JACK BITTNER
Antonio	WILL GEER

91

Balthazar	MICHAEL BORDEN
Margaret	SADA THOMPSON
Ursula	JACQUELINE BROOKES
Dogberry	LARRY GATES
Verges	ELLIS RABB

(Followed by JACK WALTZER)

Second Soldier	JAMES CAHILL
Friar Francis	PATRICK HINES

(Followed by JOHN FRID)

Sexton	JOHN FRID

"Goddess of the Night" sung by RUSSELL OBERLIN

Various Soldiers and Servants:
Benita Deutsch, Michael Kasdan, David Milton, Joe Myers, Dino Narizzano, Judith Steffan, Peter Trytler, Jack Waltzer, Michael Borden, William Woodman.

The action of the play takes place in and around the Great House of Leonato near Messina

THERE WILL BE TWO INTERMISSIONS

1958 — STRATFORD, CONNECTICUT

Premiere June 19th

HAMLET

by William Shakespeare

Directed by JOHN HOUSEMAN
Scenery by DAVID HAYS
Lighting by JEAN ROSENTHAL
Costumes by ALVIN COLT
Music by VIRGIL THOMSON

CAST OF CHARACTERS
(in order of speaking)

Bernardo	JOHN RAGIN
Francisco	WILL GEER
Horatio	EARLE HYMAN
Marcellus	MITCHELL AGRUSS
Claudius	MORRIS CARNOVSKY
Cornelius	MICHAEL KASDAN
Voltemand	SEVERN DARDEN
Laertes	JOHN COLICOS
Polonius	HIRAM SHERMAN
Gertrude	GERALDINE FITZGERALD
Hamlet	FRITZ WEAVER
Ophelia	INGA SWENSON
Ghost	JACK BITTNER
Osric	RICHARD EASTON
Rosencrantz	PATRICK HINES
Guildenstern	JAMES OLSON
Players:	
King	ELLIS RABB
Poisoner	MITCHELL AGRUSS
Queen	BARBARA BARRIE
Fortinbras	RICHARD WARING

Norwegian captain	JOHN RAGIN
Reynaldo	MICHAEL KENNEDY
A Sailor	MICHAEL KASDAN
1st Gravedigger	WILL GEER
2nd Gravedigger	WILLIAM HICKEY
Priest	JOHN RAGIN

Lords, Ladies, Switzers, Norwegian Soldiers, Players, Servants:
Richard Victor Brown, Frederick Combs, Michael Kennedy, Douglas Langley, Miller Lide, Sy Prescott, Geddeth Smith, Raymond Saint-Jacques, Don Tor, Alexander Viespi, Ellen Weston, Merryman Gatch, Katherine Geer, Joanna Merlin, Freya Mintzer.

The action of the play takes place in the Royal Palace at Elsinore.

THERE WILL BE TWO INTERMISSIONS

1958 — STRATFORD, CONNECTICUT

Premiere June 20th

A MIDSUMMER NIGHT'S DREAM

by William Shakespeare

Directed by JACK LANDAU
Scenery by DAVID HAYS
Lighting by THARON MUSSER
Costumes by THEA NEU
Music and Songs by MARC BLITZSTEIN
Sung by RUSSELL OBERLIN
Dances by GEORGE BALANCHINE

CAST OF CHARACTERS
(in order of speaking)

Theseus	JACK BITTNER
Hippolyta	NANCY WICKWIRE
Egeus	PATRICK HINES
Hermia	BARBARA BARRIE
Demetrius	JAMES OLSON
Lysander	JOHN COLICOS
Helena	INGA SWENSON
Quince	MORRIS CARNOVSKY
Bottom	HIRAM SHERMAN
Flute	WILLIAM HICKEY
Starveling	ELLIS RABB
Snout	WILL GEER
Snug	SEVERN DARDEN
Puck	RICHARD EASTON
A Fairy	JUNE ERICSON
Oberon	RICHARD WARING
Titania	JUNE HAVOC
Philostrate	EARLE HYMAN
A Master of Revels	RUSSELL OBERLIN
A Changeling Boy	SYLVESTER BRIGHT

Elves: Mark Carson, James Conway, Kenneth German, Marc Rheinfeld, Ernest Puglise, Michael Fishman.

Various Attendants: Richard Victor Brown, Frederick Combs, Michael Kennedy, Douglas Langley, Miller Lide, Sy Prescott, Geddeth Smith, Raymond Saint-Jacques, Don Tor, Alexander Viespi, Ellen Weston, Merryman Gatch, Katherine Geer, Joanna Merlin, Freya Mintzer.

The action takes place in the great hall of the palace of Theseus and in a nearby wood.

THERE WILL BE ONE INTERMISSION

1958 — STRATFORD, CONNECTICUT

Premiere July 20th

THE WINTER'S TALE

by William Shakespeare

Directed by JOHN HOUSEMAN *and* JACK LANDAU
Scenery by DAVID HAYS
Lighting by JEAN ROSENTHAL
Costumes by DOROTHY JEAKINS
Dances by GEORGE BALANCHINE
Music and Songs by MARC BLITZSTEIN

CAST OF CHARACTERS
(in order of speaking)

Archidamus	JAMES OLSON
Camillo	ELLIS RABB
Polixenes, King of Bohemia	RICHARD WARING
Leontes, King of Sicilia	JOHN COLICOS
Hermione, Queen of Sicilia	NANCY WICKWIRE
Mamillius	JAMES CONWAY
Emilia	JOANNA MERLIN
A Lady	SUSAN RISKIN
Angelo	MITCHELL AGRUSS
Antigonus	PATRICK HINES
Paulina	NANCY MARCHAND
Gaoler	MICHAEL KASDAN
Officer	SEVERN DARDEN
Cleomenes	JOHN RAGIN
Mariner	MICHAEL KASDAN
Old Shepherd	WILL GEER
Young Shepherd	WILLIAM HICKEY
Time	JACK BITTNER
Autolycus	EARLE HYMAN
Florizel	RICHARD EASTON
Perdita	INGA SWENSON
Dorcas	BARBARA BARRIE
Mopsa	JUNE ERICSON
A Shepherd	HIRAM SHERMAN
1st Gentleman	JACK BITTNER
2nd Gentleman	SEVERN DARDEN
3rd Gentleman	HIRAM SHERMAN

"The Song of the Glove" sung by RUSSELL OBERLIN

Servants, Shepherds, Shepherdesses: William Monell, Arthur Lewis, Merryman Gatch, Katherine Geer, Marilyn Greiner, Kathryn Humphries, Lynne Littman, Freya Mintzer, Barbara Joy Welt, Ellen Weston, Frederick Combs, Phelps Montgomery, Eldon Quick, Geddeth Smith, Don Tor, Alexander Viespi, Miller Lide, Donald Nation, Barbara Colton, Barbara Ann Zamborsky.

The action takes place in Sicilia, Bohemia, and again in Sicilia.

THERE WILL BE ONE INTERMISSION

Musical Director (1958) Herman Chessid

ASFTA ANNUAL SHAKESPEARE AWARDS

THESE AWARDS are presented on Shakespeare's birthday in recognition of works which stimulate appreciation of Shakespeare and the classical theatre.

1954

1. Yale University, for its 1954 Shakespeare Festival.
2. Constance Collier, for the training and guidance she has given young actors as well as stars in the interpretation of Shakespeare's plays.
3. Joyce C. Hall, president of Hallmark Cards, for sponsoring a distinguished performance by Maurice Evans in *Richard II* on NBC-TV and making the kinescope available to schools.
4. Metro-Goldwyn-Mayer— its producer, John Houseman, and its director, Joseph Mankiewicz — for *Julius Caesar.*
5. New York City Center of Music and Drama, for co-ordinating Shakespeare into its lively season of opera, ballet and drama, making Shakespeare available in New York City at popular prices—

with special recognition of the co-operative participation of Lincoln Kirstein, Jean Dalrymple, Jose Ferrer and Margaret Webster.

6. Radio Station WNYC (New York), for its annual festival presentation of Shakespeare's plays and lectures.

1955

1. Antioch College, for continued service to the works of Shakespeare by its annual presentation of a summer festival.
2. Dr. Frank Baxter, professor of English at the University of Southern California, for his CBS television program on the times and works of Shakespeare.
3. The Shakespeare Association of America, for its publication *The Shakespeare Quarterly,* which is beginning its sixth year.
4. Jack Landau and the Phoenix Theatre for their production of John Webster's *The White Devil.*
5. Helge Kökeritz and Charles Tyler Prouty, professors of English at Yale University, for their facsimile of the First Folio.
6. Judith Anderson, for her performance of Lady Macbeth in the television version of *Macbeth.*

1956

1. Professor Alfred Harbage, Harvard University, in the field of absolute scholarship, for his book *Theatre for Shakespeare.*
2. Constance Welch, in the field of education, for her instruction in Shakespearean diction at Yale.
3. Maurice Evans, in the field of television, for his production of *The Taming of the Shrew.*
4. The Shakespearewrights, in the field of Off-Broadway producing, for their versions of *Othello, Twelfth Night* and *Romeo and Juliet.*
5. Noah Greenberg of the Pro Musica Antiqua, in the field of music, for his Elizabethan Song Book and long-playing recording, "An Evening of Elizabethan Verse and Its Music."
6. Sir Laurence Olivier, in the field of motion pictures, for his production of *Richard III.*
7. The Brattle Players, in the field of legitimate theatre, for their New York City Center staging of *Othello* and *Henry IV, Part I.*
8. (A special award was given to Lawrence Langner for his "vision and effort" in behalf of the creation of the theatre at Stratford.)

1957

1. Joseph Papp, for his ingenious, persistent and enterprising series of productions of "Shakespeare under the Stars," which has made available to thousands of New Yorkers lively performances of the plays, without cost to an entranced and ever-growing public.
2. Louis B. Wright, director of the Folger Shakespeare Library, and Virginia L. Freund, for their new edition in the Folger Library General Reader's Shakespeare of *The Tragedy of King Lear.*
3. Penguin Books of Baltimore, Maryland, and publisher Harry F. Paroission, for The Pelican Shakespeare, an immaculate series of extremely well-printed and brilliantly edited texts of the plays under the editorial supervision of distinguished American scholars.
4. Professor Henry Wells of Columbia University, director of the Brander Matthews Theatre Library and Museum, who has recently caused to be built extremely beautiful and very detailed models of the Globe Theatre.
5. NBC-TV's Producers' Showcase for the telecast of *Romeo and Juliet,* which starred Claire Bloom and John Neville and was directed by Michael Benthall and Clark Jones, for one of the best shortened versions of the play available to the mass media.

1958

1. Sir Laurence Olivier, for his eminent achievement as an actor-manager, on stage and in films, in bringing Shakespeare to a popular audience.
2. Katharine Hepburn, with deepest gratitude, for her personal accomplishment and devotion to the idea of an American Shakespeare company in Stratford, Connecticut, and on tour.
3. B. Iden Payne, of the University of Texas, for continued service to the works of Shakespeare— actor, director, teacher— an inspiration for generations of theatre people.
4. Lyn Ely, for her personal accomplishment, through Theatre in Education, Inc., in bringing Shakespeare to public-school audiences.
5. William F. Friedman and Elizebeth S. Friedman, for bringing with wit, learning and patience their technical knowledge of cryptology to the academic problems of authorship in their book *The Shakespearean Cyphers Examined.*